A Cataloger's Guide to MARC Coding and Tagging for Audiovisual Material

Nancy B. Olson

MINNESOTA SCHOLARLY PRESS
DeKalb, Illinois
1993

Published by:
MINNESOTA SCHOLARLY PRESS, INC.
and Media Marketing Group
P.O. Box 611
DeKalb, Illinois 60115

Printed in the United States of America

ISBN 0-933474-49-0

This book was created electronically using Microsoft Word and Aldus PageMaker on the Apple Macintosh IIfx computer. Paste-up and layout by Sharon Olson of Apple Blossom Books.

CONTENTS

INTRODUCTION

This book contains all the examples from *Cataloging of Audiovisual Materials*, 3d edition (Minnesota Scholarly Press, 1992), with each bibliographic record coded and tagged for OCLC input. Examples are followed by comments on coding and/or tagging problems involved in the example. A chart is included that shows the coding of the 007 field for all types of material.

I have chosen to show the examples coded and tagged for OCLC input rather than showing pure MARC coding and tagging because more bibliographic records for audiovisual material are entered into the OCLC database than into the other national bibliographic utilities — WLN, RLIN, and UTLAS — and because I am familiar with OCLC as I have been a user of that utility since 1976. Each of the bibliographic utilities makes some changes to the basic MARC format, but these changes are relatively minor.

* An asterisk at the left of a line indicates a change from the cataloged example because of a new or changed authority record.

** A double asterisk at the left of a line number indicates a cataloging change to the example.

MARC Format

The development and history of the MARC format has been well documented, most recently by Walt Crawford in *MARC for Library Use: Understanding the USMARC Formats*, 2d edition (Knowledge Industry Publications).

The Network Development and MARC Standards Office at the Library of Congress issues the USMARC formats. Proposed changes to the formats are discussed, and recommendations made, at ALA annual conferences and midwinter meetings by the MARBI (Machine-Readable Bibliographic Information) Committee.

Integrated MARC Format

All MARC formats will be integrated into one format at the end of 1993. After that process is completed all codes and tags will be valid for all types of material. Some inconsistencies between formats already have been resolved in preparation for format integration. These include removing the second indicator in the 1XX fields and removing the indicators in the 260 field.

OCLC

The format documents distributed by OCLC are excellent, and contain instructions and examples to guide the user in coding and tagging bibliographic records for entry into the OCLC database. There are eight formats;

Archives and Manuscript Control

Audiovisual Media

Books

Computer Files

Maps

Scores

Serials

Sound Recordings

Each format is revised, updated, or re-issued in a new edition as needed. All will be combined into one document after format integration.

"Codes and Tags"

Each area of the bibliographic record is contained in a separate *field* in the format. A *record* contains all the fields for a cataloged item. Fields may be *fixed* or *variable*. Fixed fields are composed of separate pieces of coded information about the item, with each of the fixed fields always a standard pre-determined length. Variable fields vary in length and contain an area of the bibliographic record or coded information about the bibliographic record or about some part of it.

Each variable field is identified by a *tag*, a three-digit *code*. A code may be followed by a 1- or 2-position *indicator*. Variable fields may be divided into smaller units called *subfields*. Subfields are preceded by *subfield codes*. Each subfield code is preceded by a symbol, ǂ, called a *delimiter*.

Variable fields are grouped as follows:

1XX   Main entry headings

2XX   Title and statement of responsibility area
        Edition area
        Publication, distribution, etc., area

3XX   Physical description area

4XX   Series area

5XX   Notes area

6XX   Subject headings

7XX   Added entries
         Linking entries

8XX   Series added entries

9XX   Local-use fields

0XX   Bibliographic control numbers
         Call numbers, classification numbers
         Miscellaneous variable fields such as codes for time period involved, geographic area
                  represented, etc.

The OCLC *fixed field* contains codes for 20 or more separate bits of information taken from the leader and 008 field. The fixed field is somewhat different for each format.

The 007 field is another fixed-length field. This field contains codes for the physical description of the material. The 007 field is used for audiovisual media, sound recordings, microforms, and maps, with each format having its own values. See the accompanying chart for 007 values for each of these formats.

Because it requires 164 pages in the *USMARC Concise Bibliographic Format* to list all the 0XX-8XX fields and 120 pages to list all 1xx-8xx fields with their related indicators and subfield codes, fixed fields with their values, and variable fields, I refer the reader to the OCLC formats or the USMARC documents for complete description and explanation of the formats.

Some fields, codes, tags, etc., are optional; others are mandatory if applicable. The OCLC document *Bibliographic Input Standards* (5th ed., 1992) explains which are required for full-level (level I) input and which for minimal-level (level K) input.

OCLC User Groups

There are a number of special-interest groups that users of OCLC may join. Two of these are the Music OCLC Users Group and Online Audiovisual Catalogers, Inc.

The Music OCLC Users Group (MOUG) meets annually, usually in conjunction with the meeting of the Music Library Association. MOUG's newsletter is an occasional publication. Dues are $10.00 for an invidividual and $15.00 for an institution. Dues may be sent to:

> Ann Churukian
> Music Library, Box 38
> Vassar College
> Poughkeepsie, NY 12601

Online Audiovisual Catalogers, Inc., (OLAC) meets twice a year during the ALA Annual Conference and Midwinter Meeting and also holds a biennial conference. The OLAC publication is a quarterly newsletter. Dues are $10.00 for individuals, $16.00 for institutions. Dues may be sent to:

> Bobby Ferguson
> OLAC Treasurer
> 285 Sharp Road
> Baton Rouge, LA 70821

OLAC is for all catalogers of audiovisual materials. Members include users of all the bibliographic utilities, as well as many who do not use any of the utilities. The newsletter contains at least as much information about cataloging audiovisual materials as it does about the coding and tagging of those materials for input into OCLC or one of the other bibliographic utilities.

New *or* Edit?

Detailed information about criteria for creating new records or OCLC may be found in "When to Input a New Record", from *Bibliographic Input Standards* (OCLC, 5th ed., 1992, pp. 29-41). These guidelines are summarized as follows:

One is to *edit* a record when the bibliographic record matches but uses different cataloging rules; when one wants to make changes to reflect local cataloging adaptations or practice; when one wants to include additional information; when onee needs to reflect a change in the type of accompanying material (presence or absence of guide, poster, transparency masters, book, etc.; material that could have been removed for separate cataloging or lost or discarded before cataloging); or when one needs to correct errors.

One may create a *new* record if any of the following are different (but study the section cited above):

publisher, distributor, etc.

copyright date

date of impression, if the later impression contains textual variations

date of publication, distribution, etc.

edition

medium (videorecording vs. motion picture, sound disc vs. sound cassette, slide vs. filmstrip)

extent of item (number of reels, significant difference in number of slides, minutes, etc.)

other physical details (size, mono. vs. stereo., 8mm vs. 16mm, b&w vs. col., sd. vs. si., etc.)

series

illustrator

translator

language

manufacturer's record number for a sound recording (unless one number is the container number and
    the other is an item within the container)

accompanying material (sound disc/sound cassette)

If in doubt, do *not* create a new record.

Common 007 Code Patterns

Fimstrip, color

g ǂb o ǂd c ǂe j

Fimstrip, color, with sound cassette

g ǂb o ǂd c ǂe j ǂf b ǂg f ǂh f

Motion picture, 16 mm, color

m ǂb r ǂd c ǂe a ǂf a ǂg a ǂh d

Videocassette, VHS, 1/2 in., col.

    v ‡b f ‡d c ‡e b ‡f a ‡g h ‡h o ‡i m

Videodisc (Laservision), stereo

    v ‡b d ‡d c ‡e g ‡f a ‡g i ‡h z ‡i s

Transparencies, color, 21 x 26 cm.

    g ‡b t ‡d c ‡e k

Slides, color

    g ‡b s ‡d c ‡e j

Slides, color, sound cassette

    g ‡b s ‡d c ‡e j ‡f b ‡g f ‡h j

Sound recording, disc, stereo, 12 in.

    s ‡b d ‡d b ‡e s ‡f m ‡g e ‡h n ‡i n

Sound recording, cassette

    s ‡b s ‡d l ‡e m ‡f n ‡g j ‡h l ‡i b

Sound recording, CD

    s ‡b d ‡d o ‡e m ‡f n ‡g g ‡h m ‡i n ‡i n ‡m e

CARTOGRAPHIC MATERIALS

AACR 2 Chapter 3

Example 1: Geologic Map

```
Type:    e  Bib lvl: m  Source:    d   Lang:   eng
RecG:    a  Enc lvl: I  Govt pub: f   Ctry:   mdu
Relief: ad  Mod rec:    Base:     ^^^ Form:
Desc:    a  Indx:    1  Dat tp:    s   Dates: 1932,
 1 010
 2 040       XXX ‡c XXX
 3 007       a ‡b j ‡d c ‡e a ‡f n ‡g z ‡h n
 4 020
 5 034 1     a ‡b 62500 ‡d W0970000 ‡e W0963000 ‡f N0460000 ‡g N0453000
 6 043       n-us-mn ‡a n-us-sd ‡a n-us-nd
 7 052       4141
 8 092 0     912.776 ‡2 20
 9 090       G4141.C5 1932
10 049       XXXX
11 110 2     Geological Survey (U.S.)
12 245 10    Geologic map of the vicinity of the outlet of glacial Lake
Agassiz, North Dakota, South Dakota, and Minnesota ‡h map / ‡c U.S.
Geological Survey ; geology by Frank Leverett in part after Warren
Upham.
13 255       Scale 1:62,500. ‡c (W 97°—W 96°30´/N 46°00´—N 45°30´)
14 260       Baltimore, Md. : ‡b A. Hoen, ‡c 1932.
15 300       1 map : ‡b col. ; ‡c 89 x 63 cm.
16 490 1     Professional paper ; ‡v  161, plate 5
17 500       Relief shown by contour lines, hachures; contour interval 10
ft.
18 500       Includes index, explanation.
19 650   0   Geology ‡z Minnesota ‡x Maps.
20 650   0   Glacial lakes ‡x Maps.
21 651   0   Agassiz, Lake ‡x Maps.
22 700 10    Leverett, Frank, ‡d 1859-1943.
23 700 10    Upham, Warren, ‡d 1850-1934.
24 830   0   Geological Survey professional paper ; ‡v 161, plate 5.
```

In OCLC practice, the GMD is input without brackets.

Note the details of the 034. Map people insist this be coded, but it is time consuming to do. The degree, minute, and second symbols in subfield ‡c of field 255 each takes a sequence of keystrokes to input correctly.

For all examples —

* Changed from form appearing in *Cataloging of Audiovisual Materials,* 3d edition. LC authority file searched June 1992.

** Cataloging changed.

Example 2: Map Showing Lines of Transportation

```
Type:    e  Bib lvl: m Source:    d   Lang:    eng
RecG:    a  Enc lvl: I Govt pub:      Ctry:    cou
Relief: dg Mod rec:    Base:     ^^^ Form:
Desc:    a  Indx:    1 Dat tp:    s   Dates:  1975,
 1 010
 2 040       XXX ǂc XXX
 3 007       a ǂb j ǂd a ǂe a ǂf n ǂg z ǂh n
 4 034 1     a ǂb 63630
 5 043       n-us-co ǂa n-us-nm
 6 052       4311
 7 092 0     912.788 ǂ2 20
 8 090       G4311.P3 1975
 9 049       XXXX
10 100 1     Osterwald, Doris B.
11 245 10    Map showing lines of transportation between Antonito,
Colorado, and Chama, New Mexico ǂh map : ǂb including the Cumbres &
Toltec Scenic Railroad, State Highway 17, and the abandoned Park View
and Ft. Garland toll road / ǂc by Doris B. Osterwald.
12 255       Scale [ca. 1:63,630]
13 260       Lakewood, Co. : ǂb Western Guideways, ǂc c1975.
14 300       1 map ; ǂc 52 x 84 cm.
15 500       Relief shown by hachures and spot heights.
16 500       Includes index map and "Profile of C&TS railroad track."
17 651  0    Colorado ǂx Road maps.
18 651  0    New Mexico ǂx Road maps.
19 610 20    Cumbres and Toltec Scenic Railroad ǂx Maps.
```

    States are entered in coded form in the 043, in numeric form in the 052. Multiple states or geographic locations can be coded into the 043; the 052 includes only the single location represented by the LC classification number.

Example 3: City of Lake Crystal

```
Type:     e  Bib lvl: m Source:    d    Lang:  eng
RecG:     a  Enc lvl: I Govt pub:       Ctry:  mnu
Relief:      Mod rec:   Base:      ^^^  Form:
Desc:     a  Indx:    0 Dat tp:    s    Dates: 1985,
 1 010
 2 040         XXX ‡c XXX
 3 007         a ‡b j ‡d a ‡e a ‡f n ‡g z ‡h n
 4 034 1       a ‡b 7200
 5 043         n-us-mn
 6 052         4144 ‡a L34
 7 092 0       912.77621 ‡2 20
 9 090         G4144.L34A1 1985
10 049         XXXX
11 245 10      City of Lake Crystal, Minnesota ‡h map
12 250         Rev.
13 255         Scale [ca. 1:7,200]
14 260         [Minnesota? : ‡b s.n.], ‡c 1985.
15 300         1 map ; ‡c on sheet 43 x 56 cm.
16 500         "Revised March 1985."
17 651   0     Lake Crystal (Minn.) ‡x Maps.
```

All of the 090 shown is subfield ‡a of the Library of Congress classification number. Subfield ‡b would follow this. Map classification numbers have more parts than most other Library of Congress classification numbers.

Example 4: Mankato, Minnesota

```
Type:     e  Bib lvl: m Source:    d    Lang:  eng
RecG:     a  Enc lvl: I Govt pub:  f    Ctry:  sdu
Relief:      Mod rec:   Base:      ^^^  Form:
Desc:     a  Indx:    0 Dat tp:    s    Dates: 1986,
 1 010
 2 040         XXX ‡c XXX
 3 007         a ‡b r ‡d a ‡e a ‡f z ‡g b ‡h a
 4 034 1       a ‡b 85000
 5 043         n-us-mn
 6 052         4144 ‡b M3
 7 092 0       912.77621 ‡2 20
 8 090         G4144.M3A3 1986
 9 049         XXXX
10 110 2       Earth Resources Observation Systems.
11 245 10      [Mankato, Minnesota, area satellite image] ‡h map
12 255         Scale [ca. 1:85,000]
13 260         [Sioux Falls, S.D. : ‡b U.S. Geological Survey, EROS Data
Center, ‡c 1989]
14 300         1 remote-sensing image ; ‡c 23 x 23 cm.
15 500         Title supplied by cataloger.
16 500         Sheet dated 8-8-86.
17 500         "[Roll] 228-[frame] 14 449416 HAP 85."
18 651   0     Mankato (Minn.) ‡x Photographs from space.
```

Example 5: Ohio Covered Bridges

```
Type:     e  Bib lvl: m Source:    d    Lang:    eng
RecG:     a  Enc lvl: I Govt pub:      Ctry:    ohu
Relief:      Mod rec:    Base:      ^^^ Form:
Desc:     a  Indx:    0 Dat tp:    s    Dates: 1972,
 1 010
 2 040        XXX ǂc XXX
 3 007        a ǂb j ǂd m ǂe a ǂf n ǂg z ǂh n
 4 034 0      a
 5 043        n-us-oh
 6 052        4081
 7 092 0      912.771
 8 090        G4081.P24 1972
 9 049        XXXX
10 245 00     Ohio covered bridges ǂh map
11 255        Scale indeterminable.
12 260        Columbus, Ohio : ǂb Ohio Historical Society, ǂc 1972.
13 300        1 map : ǂb col. ; ǂc 42 x 37 on sheet 43 x 55 cm. + ǂe 1
sheet of additions, deletions & corrections.
14 500        Locates covered bridges existing in Ohio in 1972.
15 500        "Published ... with the cooperation and assistance of the
Ohio Covered Bridge Committee."
16 500        Sheet of additions, deletions, and corrections dated "1972,
revised 1984."
17 500        Includes inset maps: W. Washington County -- N. Perry County
-- Cent. Preble County.
18 500        Sketches of truss designs and list of covered bridges on
verso.
19 650   0    Covered bridges ǂz Ohio ǂx Maps.
20 710 20     Ohio Historical Society.
21 710 20     Ohio Covered Bridge Committee.
```

The inset map note could be coded as a partial contents note, but it generates a print constant that I didn't want to use.

Example 6: The National Road

```
Type:      e  Bib lvl: m  Source:    d   Lang:   eng
RecG:      a  Enc lvl: I  Govt pub:      Ctry:   ohu
Relief:       Mod rec:    Base:      ^^^ Form:
Desc:      a  Indx:    0  Dat tp:    q   Dates: 1980,1983
   1 010
   2 040        XXX ‡c XXX
   3 007        a ‡b j ‡d a ‡e a ‡f n ‡g z ‡h n
   4 034  0     a
   5 043        n-us-mn
   6 052        4081
   7 092        912.771 ‡2 20
   8 090        G4081.P2 1940
   9 049        XXXX
  10 245  04    The National Road ‡h map : ‡b [eastern United States]
  11 255        Scale indeterminable.
  12 300        1 map ; ‡c 17 x 24 cm.
  13 500        Inset: Map of United States Route 40.
* 14 651   0    Cumberland Road ‡x Maps.
  15 773  0     ‡7 c2am ‡t The National Road in song and story. ‡d Columbus,
Ohio : Ohio Historical Society, [198-]. ‡w (OCoLC)nnnnnnnn
```

Field 773 is coded and tagged as shown. It will generate the "In" analytic note on a catalog card.

Example 7: Capitol Hill

```
Type:    e  Bib lvl: m Source:    d    Lang:   eng
RecG:    a  Enc lvl: I Govt pub:        Ctry:   mdu
Relief:     Mod rec:   Base:      ^^^ Form:   m
Desc:    a  Indx:    0 Dat tp:  s    Dates: 1988,
 1 010
 2 040       XXX ‡c XXX
 3 007       a ‡b j ‡d c ‡e e ‡f z ‡g z ‡h n
 4 034 0     a
 5 043       n-us-dc
 6 052       3851
 7 092 0     912.753 ‡2 20
 8 090       G3851.A7
 9 049       XXXX
10 100 1     Weidel, Joseph W.
11 245 10    Capitol Hill and the Mall ‡h map : ‡b [Washington, D.C.] /
‡c J.W. Wiedel.
12 255       Scale indeterminable.
13 260       [Ellicott City, Md. : ‡b Schuyler Fonaroff Associates, ‡c
1988]
14 300       1 map (print, braille, and tactile) : ‡b col., plastic ; ‡c
35 x 48 cm. + ‡e 1 brochure.
15 500       "Produced for and funded by the United States Department of
Education, Office of Special Education and Rehabilitative Service."
16 500       Raised outlines for buildings, raised dotted lines for
streets; street names and building symbols in braille and large print.
17 500       Brochure, "The tactile capital," describes exhibit,
photographs, maps, and model of the Tactile Capital project for the
blind, visually impaired, and others with disabilities.
18 651 0    Washington (D.C.) ‡x Maps for the blind.
19 651 0    Washington (D.C.) ‡x Maps for the visually handicapped.
20 650 0    Public buildings ‡z Washington (D.C.) ‡x Maps.
21 710 20   United States. ‡b Office of Special Education and
Rehabilitative Service.
```

One could use a reference source to obtain coordinates for field 034.

Example 8: New Mexico in 3-D

```
Type:    e  Bib lvl: m Source:    d   Lang:    eng
RecG:    a  Enc lvl: I Govt pub:      Ctry:    cou
Relief: gz  Mod rec:   Base:     ^^^ Form:    m
Desc:    a  Indx:     0 Dat tp:    s   Dates: 1975,
 1 010
 2 040      XXX ‡c XXX
 3 007      a ‡b q ‡d c ‡e e ‡f z ‡g z ‡h n
 4 034 1    a ‡b 1584000
 5 043      n-us-nm
 6 052      4321
 7 090      G4321.C18 1975
 8 092 0    912.789 ‡2 20
 9 049      XXXX
10 110 2    Kistler Graphics, inc.
11 245 00   New Mexico in 3-D ‡h map / ‡c produced by Kistler Graphics.
12 255      Scale [ca. 1:1,584,000]. 1 in. to ca. 25 miles. Vertical
scale [ca. 1:192,000]
13 260      Denver, Colo. : ‡b Kistler, ‡c 1975.
14 300      1 relief model : ‡b col., plastic ; ‡c 42 x 38 cm.
15 500      Relief shown by raised areas, spot heights.
16 500      Base map by Jeppesen & Co., 1964, "revised 5-68."
17 651  0   New Mexico ‡x Relief models.
18 710 20   Jeppesen and Company.
```

All these statements of scale go in one subfield in field 255.

Example 9: Minnesota Outdoor Atlas

```
Type: a Bib lvl: m Source:   d Lang:   eng
Repr:    Enc lvl: I Conf pub: 0 Ctry:   mnu
Indx: 0 Mod rec:   Govt pub:   Cont:
Desc: a Int lvl:   Festschr: 0 Illus: ab
        F/B: 0     Dat tp:   s Dates: 1979,
 1 010
 2 040       XXX ǂc XXX
 3 020       0932880002
 4 034 0     a
 5 043       n-us-mn
 6 052       4140
 7 092 0     912.776 ǂ2 20
 9 090       G1426.E63
10 049       XXXX
11 100 1     Miles, Catherine H.
12 245 10    Minnesota outdoor atlas : ǂb a guide to state and national
recreation lands in Minnesota / ǂc by Catherine H. Miles and Donald P.
Yaeger ; two-color photographs by D. Yaeger.
13 255       Scales vary.
14 260       [Minnesota : ǂb s.n.] ; ǂa West St. Paul, Minn. : ǂb
Distributed by The Map Store, ǂc c1979.
15 300       1 atlas (232 p.) : ǂb ill. (some col.), ǂc col. maps ; 44
cm.
16 500       Scale of most counties ca. 1:210,000.
16 650   0   Outdoor recreation ǂz Minnesota ǂx Maps.
17 651   0   Minnesota ǂx Public lands ǂx Maps.
18 700 10    Yaeger, Donald P.
```

An atlas is entered on the book format workform.

In field 260 the place and name of distribution are separately subfielded; subfields ǂa and ǂb are repeated.

Example 10: Atlas of Crawford County, Iowa

```
Type: a Bib lvl: m Source:    d Lang:    eng
Repr:    Enc lvl: I Conf pub: 0 Ctry:    iau
Indx: 0 Mod rec:    Govt pub:    Cont:
Desc: a Int lvl:    Festschr: 0 Illus: b
         F/B:       0 Dat tp:    s Dates: 1920,
   1 010
   2 040      XXX ǂc XXX
   3 034 0    a
   4 043      n-us-ia
   5 052      4153 ǂa C9
   5 092 0    912.77745 ǂ2 20
   6 090      G1433.C9
   7 049      XXXX
*  8 110 2    Anderson Publishing Company.
   9 245 10   Atlas of Crawford County, Iowa : ǂb containing maps of
townships of the county, maps of state, United States, and world,
farmers directory, analysis of the system of U.S. land surveys.
  10 255      Scales vary.
  11 260      Des Moines, Iowa : ǂb Anderson Pub. Co., ǂc c1920.
  12 300      1 atlas : ǂb col. maps ; ǂc 46 cm.
  13 651 0    Crawford County (Iowa) ǂx Maps.
  14 650 0    Real property ǂz Iowa ǂz Crawford County ǂx Maps.
```

No GMD is used for atlases.

Example 11: Replogle Stereo Relief Globe

```
Type:    e Bib lvl: m Source:    d    Lang:    eng
RecG:    d Enc lvl: I Govt pub:       Ctry:    ilu
Relief: z Mod rec:    Base:      ^^^ Form:
Desc:    a Indx:     0 Dat tp:    q    Dates: 1970,1979
   1 010
   2 040      XXX ǂc XXX
   3 007      d ǂb c ǂd c ǂe u ǂf u
   4 034 1    a ǂb 41849600
   5 052      3171
   6 090      G3171.C18 1970
   7 092 0    912 ǂ2 20
   8 049      XXXX
*  9 110 2    Replogle Globes.
  10 245 10   Replogle stereo relief globe ǂh globe
  11 255      Scale 1:41,849,600.
  12 260      Chicago, Ill. : ǂb Replogle Globes, ǂc [197-]
  13 300      1 globe : ǂb col, on metal stand ; ǂc 12 in. in diam.
  14 500      Relief shown by raised areas.
  15 650 0    Globes.
```

Globes and all other cartographic items except atlases are coded as Type "e" material.

Example 12: Map of United States

```
Type:        r Bib lvl: m Source:     d Lang:    eng
Type mat: g Enc lvl: I Govt pub:    Ctry:    pau
Int lvl:  d Mod rec:    Tech:     n Leng:    nnn
Desc:        a Accomp:    Dat tp:   s Dates: 1963,
 1 010
 2 040       XXX ǂc XXX
 3 043       n-us-
 4 092 0     912.73
 5 090       G3701.F1
 6 049       XXXX
 7 245 00    Map of United States ǂh game / ǂc designed exclusively for
Nashco by David B. Tibbetts.
 8 260       Scranton, PA : ǂb Nashco Products, ǂc 1963.
 9 300       1 puzzle (55 pieces) : ǂb wood, col. ; ǂc 41 x 60 cm.
10 500       Wooden tray with depressed area into which state and Great
Lakes pieces are to be assembled; name of each state and its capital,
and each lake, is on tray in correct location; pieces not labeled.
11 500       Scale not given.
12 500       "All puzzles are hand cut and hand colored with leadfree,
non-toxic paint."
13 500       "Not recommended for children under 3 years of age."
14 651 0     United States ǂx Maps.
15 650 0     Puzzles.
16 700 11    Tibbetts, David B.
17 710 21    Nashco Products, Inc.
```

This record for a game does not have a field 007. Games are input on the audiovisual workform.

Example 13: Global Pursuit

```
Type:       r Bib lvl: m Source:    d Lang:    eng
Type mat: g Enc lvl: I Govt pub:    Ctry:    dcu
Int lvl:  e Mod rec:   Tech:      n Leng:    nnn
Desc:       a Accomp:    Dat tp:   s Dates: 1987,
 1 010
 2 040       XXX ‡c XXX
 3 007       a ‡b j ‡d c ‡e a ‡f u ‡g u ‡h n
 3 092 0     795.43
 4 090       GV1485
 5 049       XXXX
 6 245 00  Global pursuit ‡h game / ‡c National Geographic.
 7 260       Washington, D.C. : ‡b National Geographic Society, ‡c c1987.
 8 300       1 game (various pieces) ; ‡c in box 26 x 42 x 8 cm.
 9 500       "A fun-filled geography game for the whole family."
10 500       Map cards are five-sided; each set forms a complete
dodecahedron; include political map, physical map, map of natural
resources, and map of explorations.
11 500       Map: The world / produced by the Cartographic Division,
National Geographic Society. Scale 1:67,200,000 ; Van der Grinten proj.
Washington, D.C. : The Society, c1987. 1 map : col., plastic ; 46 x 61
cm. "Prepared specially for National Geographic's Global pursuit game."
Insets: Language groups -- Religions (both Eckert equal-area proj.) --
Antarctica -- Arctic Ocean.
12 520       Player must answer questions and correctly assemble map
pieces to earn points. For 2-6 players or teams.
13 505 0   Includes 6 decks trivia cards, 4 sets map cards, 12-sided
die, plastic tokens, manual, and wall map.
14 650   0  Geographical recreations.
15 710 21  National Geographic Society (U.S.)
16 740 01  National Geographic Global pursuit.
```

With format integration we could add a field 034 for the map.

The added entrty for National Geographic Society includes the qualifier "(U.S.)" There is no subfield code before a qualifier added to a personal or corporate name. These can cause searching problems in some catalogs. If a user must key in an exact name to get a response, the user will not be likely to know what, if any, qualifier may have been added. Some catalogs allow searches that ignore the qualifier. A term or keyword search will always work on these entries.

Example 14: Globe Coffee Set

```
Type:        r Bib lvl: m Source:     d Lang:     eng
Type mat:  r Enc lvl: I Govt pub:     Ctry:    xxu
Int lvl:   g Mod rec:    Tech:      n Leng:    nnn
Desc:        a Accomp:     Dat tp:    q Dates:  1980,1986
 1 010
 2 040      XXX ‡c XXX
 3 092 0    641.877
 4 090      TX817.C6
 5 049      XXXX
 6 245 00   [Globe coffee set] ‡h realia
 7 260      [United States] : ‡b Nescaf´e, ‡c [198-]
 8 300      1 coffee pot, 2 cups : ‡b glass ; ‡c 16, 7 cm. high.
 9 500      Globe-shaped cups and coffee pot, distributed by Nescaf´e as
premiums.
10 500      Title supplied by cataloger.
11 500      Continents and latitude and longitude lines etched on glass
surface. Latitude lines used as indication of capacity of coffee pot;
marked "Two, four, six."
12 500      Molded on underside of cups: "Taste your way, Nescaf´e."
13 650  0   Coffee brewing ‡x Equipment and supplies.
14 710 21   Nescaf´e (Firm)
```

A diacritic is input in the space preceding the letter over or under which it appears when printed.

SOUND RECORDINGS

AACR 2 Chapter 6

Example 15: Macbeth

```
Type:     i Bib lvl: m Source: d  Lang:   eng
Repr:       Enc lvl: I Format: n  Ctry:   nyu
Accomp:     Mod rec:   Comp:   nn LTxt:   d
Desc:     a Int lvl:   Dat tp: s  Dates:  1963,
 1 040      XXX ǂc XXX
 2 007      s ǂb d ǂd b ǂe m ǂf m ǂg e ǂh n ǂi n
 3 028 02   TC 1167 ǂb Caedmon
 4 090      PR2823
 5 092 0    822.33 ǂ2 20
 6 049      XXXX
 7 100 1    Shakespeare, William, ǂd 1564-1616.
 8 240 10   Macbeth. ǂk Selections
 9 245 10   Great scenes from Macbeth ǂh sound recording / ǂc
Shakespeare.
10 260      New York, N.Y. : ǂb Caedmon, ǂc [1963]
11 300      1 sound disc : ǂb analog, 33 1/3 rpm ; ǂc 12 in. + ǂe
1 booklet (24 p. ; 28 cm.).
12 511 0    Anthony Quayle, Gwen Ffrangcon Davies, Stanley
Holloway, and cast ; directed by Howard Sackler.
13 500      "From American Shakespeare 7th annual festival award
winning series"--Album cover.
14 650 0    English drama ǂy Early modern and Elizabethan, 1500-
1600.
15 700 10   Quayle, Anthony, ǂd 1913-
16 700 10   Davies, Gwen Ffrangcon.
17 700 10   Holloway, Stanley.
18 700 10   Sackler, Howard.
19 740 01   Macbeth.
```

The field 740 is needed to generate an access point for the partial title. The 028 field generates the note for the record manufacturer's number.

"Accomp" is not coded unless the material for which a code may be assigned is (1) mentioned in a note and (2) substantial or unique and could not be found in a standard reference work.

For all examples —

* Changed from form appearing in *Cataloging of Audiovisual Materials*, 3d edition. LC authority file searched June 1992.

** Cataloging changed.

Example 16: Loyalties

```
Type:     i Bib lvl: m Source: d  Lang:   eng
Repr:       Enc lvl: I Format: n  Ctry:   nyu
Accomp:     Mod rec:  Comp:   nn LTxt:   t
Desc:     a Int lvl:   Dat tp: s  Dates: 1970,
 1 040      XXX ǂc XXX
 2 007      s ǂb d ǂd b ǂe s ǂf m ǂg e ǂh n ǂi n
 3 028      FS 12004 ǂb Scholastic Magazines
 4 090      BJ1533.L8
 5 092 0    179.9 ǂ2 20
 6 049      XXXX
 7 245 00   Loyalties ǂh sound recording : ǂb whose side are you
on? / ǂc produced by Sheila Turner and Robert Mack.
 8 260      [New York] : ǂb Scholastic Magazines, ǂc c1970.
 9 300      1 sound disc (ca. 44 min.) : ǂb analog, 33 1/3 rpm,
stereo. ; ǂc 12 in.
10 490 0    "A Contact record."
11 500      Notes on container.
12 520      People talking about experiences, ideas, and problems
in their own lives involving their loyalties.
13 505 0    General introduction (2 min.) -- Street gang (9 min.,
43 sec.) -- Antiwar demonstration (5 min., 16 sec.) -- Viet Nam
veterans (5 min., 46 sec.) -- Frank Garcia (5 min., 30 sec.) --
Rachel Ortiz (14 min., 30 sec.).
14 650  0   Loyalty.
15 650  8   Loyalty ǂx Case studies.
16 700 10   Turner, Sheila.
17 700 10   Mack, Robert.
18 710 21   Scholastic Magazines, Inc.
19 740 01   Loyalties, whose side are you on?
20 740 01   Whose side are you on?
```

In the fixed field LTxT is coded "t" for interviews.

Example 17: Great American Women's Speeches

```
Type:     i Bib lvl: m Source: d  Lang:   eng
Repr:       Enc lvl: I Format: n  Ctry:   nyu
Accomp:     Mod rec:   Comp:   nn LTxt:   1
Desc:     a Int lvl:   Dat tp: s  Dates:  1973,
   1 010      72-750999
   2 040      XXX ǂc XXX
   3 007      s ǂb d ǂd b ǂe s ǂf m ǂg e ǂh n ǂi n
   4 028 02   TC 2067 ǂb Caedmon
   5 043      n-us---
   6 045      w4x0
   7 090      HQ1423
   8 092 0    324.623 ǂ2 20
   9 049      XXXX
* 10 100 1    Heckart, Eileen, ǂd 1919-
  11 245 10   Great American women's speeches ǂh sound recording
  12 260      New York, N.Y. : ǂb Caedmon, ǂc p1973.
  13 300      2 sound discs (ca. 70 min.) : ǂb analog, 33 1/3 rpm,
stereo. ; ǂc 12 in.
  14 511 0    Read by Eileen Heckart, Claudia McNeil, and Mildred
Natwick ; edited by Sharon Donovan.
  15 500      Notes by Sharon Donovan on container.
  16 505 0    Declaration of sentiments and resolutions : the first
Woman's Rights Convention, Seneca Falls, New York, July 19-20,
1848 (11 min., 15 sec.) -- A demand for the political rights of
women / Lucretia Mott (7 min., 57 sec.) -- Ain't I a woman? /
Sojourner Truth (2 min., 40 sec.) -- Remove the legal shackles
from woman / Ernestine Potowski Rose (5 min., 7 sec.) -- The women
want their rights / Sojourner Truth (5 min.) -- Disappointment is
the lot of women / Lucy Stone (4 min., 47 sec.) -- Address to the
New York State Legislature (1860) / Elizabeth Cady Stanton (7
min., 54 sec.) -- Are women persons? / Susan B. Anthony (4 min.,
12 sec.) -- Womanliness (3 min., 13 sec.) ; Solitude of self (6
min., 5 sec.) / Elizabeth Cady Stanton -- Address to the National
Woman Suffrage Association, Washington, D.C., 1902 / Carrie
Chapman Catt (12 min., 3 sec.) -- Working women need the ballot /
Florence Kelley (5 min., 27 sec.) -- Emotionalism in politics? /
Anna Howard Shaw (3 min.) -- "We who like the children of Israel"
/ Elizabeth Cady Stanton (1 min., 13 sec.).
  17 650  0   Feminists.
  18 650  0   Social reformers ǂz United States.
  19 650  0   Women ǂx Suffrage.
  20 650  8   Feminism.
  21 650  8   Women ǂx Civil rights.
  22 650  8   Women ǂx Suffrage.
  23 700 10   Donovan, Sharon.
  24 700 10   McNeil, Claudia.
* 25 700 10   Natwick, Mildred, ǂd 1908-
  26 700 12   Mott, Lucretia, ǂd 1793-1880. ǂt Demand for the
political rights of women. ǂf 1973.
  27 700 12   Truth, Sojourner, ǂd 1797-1883. ǂt Ain't I a woman? ǂf
1973.
```

(Continued on next page)

* 28 700 12   Rose, Ernestine L. ǂq (Ernestine Louise), ǂd 1810-
1892. ǂt Remove the legal shackles from woman. ǂf 1973.
  29 700 12   Truth, Sojourner, ǂd 1797-1883. ǂt Women want their
rights! ǂf 1973.
  30 700 12   Stone, Lucy, ǂd 1818-1893. ǂt Disappointment is the
lot of woman. ǂf 1973.
  31 700 12   Stanton, Elizabeth Cady, ǂd 1815-1902. ǂt Address to
the New York State Legislature. ǂf 1973.
* 32 700 12   Anthony, Susan B. ǂq (Susan Brownell), ǂd 1820-1906.
ǂt Are women persons? ǂf 1973.
  33 700 12   Stanton, Elizabeth Cady, ǂd 1815-1902. ǂt Womanliness.
ǂf 1973.
  34 700 12   Stanton, Elizabeth Cady, ǂd 1815-1902. ǂt Solitude of
self. ǂf 1973.
  35 700 12   Catt, Carrie Chapman, ǂd 1859-1947. ǂt Address to the
National American Woman Suffrage Association. ǂf 1973.
  36 700 12   Kelley, Florence, ǂd 1859-1932. ǂt Working women need
the ballot. ǂf 1973.
  37 700 12   Shaw, Anna Howard, ǂd 1847-1919. ǂt Emotionalism in
politics. ǂf 1973.
  38 700 12   Stanton, Elizabeth Cady, ǂd 1815-1902. ǂt We who like
the children of Israel. ǂf 1973.
  39 730 02   Declaration of sentiments and resolutions. ǂf 1973.

     We may use a field 045 for the time period represented, 1840-1902.
     Note the Library of Congress control number is recorded in field 010.
     The author-uniform title added entries are coded as shown. Those with an asterisk were changed after a recent
authority file search.

Example 18: Coronation Service

```
Type:      i Bib lvl: m Source: d  Lang:    eng
Repr:        Enc lvl: I Format: n Ctry:    enk
Accomp:      Mod rec:   Comp:    nn LTxt:    gh
Desc:      a Int lvl:   Dat tp: s  Dates:   1953,
 1 040      XXX ‡c XXX
 2 007      s ‡b d ‡d b ‡e m ‡f m ‡g e ‡h n ‡i n
 3 028 02   ALP 1056--ALP 1058 ‡b EMI Records
 4 043      e-uk---
 5 045 0    ‡b d19530602
 6 090      DA112
 7 092 0    941.085 ‡2 20
 8 049      XXXX
 9 110 2    Church of England.
10 240 10   Coronation service
11 245 14   The coronation service of Her Majesty, Queen Elizabeth
II ‡h sound recording : ‡b Westminster Abbey, 2nd June, 1953.
12 260      London : ‡b EMI Records, ‡c [1953]
13 300      3 sound discs (120 min.) : ‡b analog, 33 1/3 rpm,
mono. ; ‡c 12 in. + ‡e 1 set of program notes (4 p. ; 26 cm.)
14 500      Service conducted by G. Fisher, Archbishop of
Canterbury.
15 511 0    Commentators: John Snagge, Howard Marshall.
16 600 00   Elizabeth ‡b II, ‡c Queen of Great Britain, ‡d 1926-
‡x Coronation.
17 700 00   Elizabeth ‡b II, ‡c Queen of Great Britain, ‡d 1926-
* 18 700 20   Fisher of Lambeth, Geoffrey Francis Fisher, ‡c Baron,
‡d 1887-1972.
19 700 10   Snagge, John.
20 700 10   Marshall, Howard.
```

Note the treatment of the range of numbers in field 028. Field 045 is coded for the exact date of the event/recording; the first indicator "0" is for a single date.

Example 19: They Chose America

```
Type:     i Bib lvl: m Source: d  Lang:   eng
Repr:       Enc lvl: I Format: n  Ctry:   nju
Accomp:     Mod rec:    Comp:   nn LTxt:   t
Desc:     a Int lvl:    Dat tp: s  Dates: 1975
 1 040      XXX ǂc XXX
 2 007      s ǂb s ǂd l ǂe m ǂf n ǂg j ǂh l ǂi c
 3 043      n-us---
 4 045      x0x6
 5 090      E184.A1
 6 092 0    325.73 ǂ2 20
 7 049      XXXX
 8 245 00   They chose America ǂh sound recording
 9 260      Princeton, N.J. : ǂb Visual Education, ǂc c1975.
10 300      12 sound cassettes : ǂb analog.
11 511 0    Producer-director: Scott McDade.
12 500      In two containers.
13 500      Notes on containers.
14 520      Interviews with Jewish immigrants and with immigrants
from China, Ireland, Italy, Mexico, Poland, Cuba, Germany, Greece,
Hungary, Japan, Finland, Norway, Denmark, and Sweden, who arrived
in America between 1902 and 1968.
15 651  0   United States ǂx Emigration and immigration.
16 651  8   United States ǂx Immigration and emigration.
17 700 10   McDade, Scott.
18 710 20   Visual Education Corporation.
```

Example 20: Mothers and Daughters

```
Type:     i Bib lvl: m Source: d  Lang:    eng
Repr:       Enc lvl: I Format: n  Ctry:    cau
Accomp:     Mod rec:   Comp:   nn LTxt:    1
Desc:     a Int lvl:   Dat tp: q  Dates: 1970,1979
 1 040      XXX ǂc XXX
 2 007      s ǂb t ǂd l ǂe m ǂf n ǂg j ǂh l ǂi c
 3 028 02   BC 0860 ǂb Pacifica Tape Library
 4 090      HQ755.85
 5 092 0    306.8743 ǂ2 20
 6 049      XXXX
 7 245 00   Mothers and daughters ǂh sound recording
 8 260      Los Angeles, Calif. : ǂb Pacifica Tape Library, ǂc
[197-]
 9 300      1 sound cassette (38 min.) : ǂb analog.
10 520      Explores relationships between mothers and daughters
through words of poets, writers, and suffragettes.
11 650  0   Mothers and daughters.
12 650  0   Daughters.
13 650  8   Girls.
14 650  8   Mothers.
15 650  8   Parent and child.
16 710 20   Pacifica Tape Library.
```

The questionable date is coded as shown in the fixed field "Dates" and "Dat tp."

Example 21: Cardiology

```
Type:     i Bib lvl: m Source: d  Lang:    eng
Repr:       Enc lvl: I Format: n  Ctry:    nyu
Accomp:     Mod rec:   Comp:   nn LTxt:    i
Desc:     a Int lvl:   Dat tp: s Dates: 1967
 1 040      XXX ǂc XXX
 2 007      s ǂb t ǂd m ǂe m ǂf n ǂg b ǂh m ǂi b
 3 090      R728.8
 4 092 0    651.3741 ǂ2 19
 5 049      XXXX
 6 100 1    Root, Kathleen Berger, ǂd 1891-
 7 245 10   Cardiology ǂh sound recording / ǂc Root and Byers.
 8 260      New York : ǂb Gregg, ǂc [1967?]
 9 300      1 sound tape reel : ǂb analog, 3 3/4 ips ; ǂc 5 in.
10 440  0   Gregg text tapes, medical dictation & transcription
11 500      Track 1: 50, 60, 70, 60 wpm from: The medical
secretary, terminology and transcription. 3rd ed. New York :
McGraw-Hill, c1967.
12 500      Track 2: 60 wpm from: Medical typing practice. 2nd ed.
New York : McGraw-Hill, c1967.
13 650  0   Dictation (Office practice)
14 650  0   Medical shorthand ǂx Study and teaching.
15 650  8   Shorthand ǂx Study and teaching.
16 700 10   Byers, Edward Elmer.
```

Field 650 does not have a subfield code before the parenthetical qualifier.

Example 22: The Mysterious Traveler

```
Type:     i Bib lvl: m Source: d  Lang:   eng
Repr:       Enc lvl: I Format: n  Ctry:   nyu
Accomp:     Mod rec:    Comp:   nn LTxt:   f
Desc:     a Int lvl:   Dat tp: q  Dates:  1970,1979
 1 040      XXX ‡c XXX
 2 007      d ‡b t ‡d o ‡e m ‡f n ‡g c ‡h m ‡i b
 3 033 1    19461229 ‡a 19470727
 4 090      PN3448.S45
 5 092 0    808.838762 ‡2 20
 6 049      XXXX
 7 245 04   The Mysterious traveler ‡h sound recording
 8 260      Croton-on-Hudson, N.Y. : ‡b Radio Yesteryear, ‡c [197-
]
 9 300      1 sound tape reel : ‡b analog, 7 1/2 ips ; ‡c 7 in.
10 500      Radio programs from Dec. 29, 1946, and July 27, 1947,
that "journey into the realm of the strange and the terrifying."
11 650  0   Science fiction.
12 650  8   Science fiction ‡x Collections.
13 710 20   Radio Yesteryear (Firm)
```

We may use a field 033 based on any information in the bibliographic record. Here it is used for the performance dates. The first indicator "1" is for multiple single dates.

Example 23: Funeral of Sir Winston Churchill.

```
Type:     i Bib lvl: m Source: d  Lang:   eng
Repr:       Enc lvl: I Format: n  Ctry:   dcu
Accomp:     Mod rec:    Comp:   nn LTxt:   g
Desc:     a Int lvl:   Dat tp: s  Dates:  1965
 1 040      XXX ‡c XXX
 2 007      s ‡b z ‡d b ‡e m ‡f m ‡g z ‡h n ‡i n
 3 045 0    ‡b d19650130
 4 090      DA566.9.C5
 5 092 0    941.0856 ‡2 20
 6 049      XXXX
 7 245 04   The Funeral of Sir Winston Churchill ‡h sound
recording : ‡b London, January 30, 1965 : with excerpts from his
speeches.
 8 300      1 sound sheet between p. 198 and 199 : ‡b analog, 33
1/3 rpm, mono. ; ‡c 7 in.
 9 511 3    David Brinkley.
10 600 10   Churchill, Winston, ‡c Sir, ‡d 1874-1965 ‡x Funeral.
11 600 18   Churchill, Winston, ‡c Sir, ‡d 1874-1965 ‡x Funeral.
12 700 10   Churchill, Winston, ‡c Sir, ‡d 1874-1965.
13 700 10   Brinkley, David.
14 773 0    ‡7 nnas ‡t National geographic. ‡g Vol. 128, no. 2
(Aug. 1965) ‡w (OCoLC) 1643684
```

This is done as an "In" analytic. Field 773 will generate the "In" note. Indicator "3" in field 511 generates the print constant "Narrator:"

Example 24: Mighty and Majestic Birds

```
Type:     i Bib lvl: m Source: d  Lang:    eng
Repr:       Enc lvl: I Format: n  Ctry:    xxu
Accomp:     Mod rec:  Comp:    nn LTxt:    s
Desc:     a Int lvl:  Dat tp: s  Dates: 1977
  1 040       XXX ǂc XXX
  2 007       s ǂb z ǂd z ǂe m ǂf u ǂg z ǂh n ǂi n
  3 090       QL698.5
  4 092 0     598.259 ǂ2 20
  5 049       XXXX
  6 245 00    Mighty and majestic birds ǂh sound recording
  7 260       [United States] : ǂb National Audubon Society, ǂc
c1977.
  8 300       10 sound disc cards : ǂb analog ; ǂc 13 x 7 cm.
  9 440 0     Audible Audubon ; ǂv set B
 10 500       For use on Microphonograph manufactured by Microsonics
Corporation.
 11 520       Each card has copy of painting by Allan Brooks on one
side; notes covered by clear plastic sound recording on the other.
Sound recordings include brief description of the bird and its
calls, followed by some of the bird calls.
 12 505 0     Red-shouldered hawk -- Red-tailed hawk -- American
kestrel -- Chuck-will's-widow -- Great horned owl -- Barred owl --
Whip-poor-will -- Long-eared owl -- Bald eagle -- Screech owl.
 13 650  0    Bird-song.
 14 650  8    Bird song.
*15 700 10    Brooks, Allan, ǂd 1869-1986.
 16 710 20    National Audubon Society.
```

Field 007 contains several instances of "z" for "other." When we do not know the exact place, but do know it was produced/published in the United States, the fixed field "Ctry" is coded "xxu" indicating state is unknown.

Example 25: Wynton Marsalis

```
Type:    j Bib lvl: m Source: d  Lang:  N/A
Repr:      Enc lvl: I Format: n  Ctry:  nyu
Accomp:    Mod rec:   Comp:   jz LTxt:
Desc:    a Int lvl:   Dat tp: s  Dates: 1982
 1 010
 2 040      XXX ‡c XXX
 3 007      s ‡b d ‡d f ‡e s ‡f n ‡g g ‡h n ‡i n ‡m e
 4 024 1    7464375742
 5 028 02   CK 37574 ‡b CBS
 6 090      M1366
 7 092 0    781.65 ‡b 20
 8 049      XXXX
 9 100 1    Marsalis, Wynton, ‡d 1961-
10 245 10   Wynton Marsalis ‡h sound recording
11 260      N[ew] Y[ork], N.Y. : ‡b CBS, ‡c p1982.
12 300      1 sound disc : ‡b digital, stereo. ; 4 3/4 in. + ‡e 1
set of program notes.
13 500      Jazz ensembles.
14 511 0    Wynton Marsalis, trumpet, with Branford Marsalis,
saxophone ; Herbie Hancock or Kenny Kirkland, piano ; Clarence
Seay, Charles Fambrough, or Ron Carter, double bass ; Jeff Watts
or Tony Williams, drums.
15 500      Compact disc.
16 500      Program notes by Stanley Crouch inserted in container.
17 505 0    Father Time / W. Marsalis -- I'll be there when the
time is right / H. Hancock -- RJ / R. Carter -- Hesitation / W.
Marsalis -- Sister Cheryl / T. Williams -- Who can I turn to (when
nobody needs me) / L. Bricusse-A. Newley -- Twilight / W.
Marsalis.
18 650  0   Jazz ensembles.
19 650  8   Jazz ensembles ‡x Collected works.
20 650  8   Jazz music ‡x Collected works.
21 700 10   Marsalis, Branford.
22 700 10   Hancock, Herbie, ‡d 1940-
23 700 10   Kirkland, Kenny.
24 700 10   Seay, Clarence.
25 700 10   Fambrough, Charles.
26 700 10   Carter, Ron, ‡d 1937-
*27 700 10   Watts, Jeffrey.
28 700 10   Williams, Tony, ‡d 1945-
29 700 12   Marsalis, Wynton, ‡d 1961- ‡t Father Time. ‡f 1982.
30 700 12   Hancock, Herbie, ‡d 1940- ‡t I'll be there when the
time is right. ‡f 1982.
31 700 12   Carter, Ron, ‡d 1937- ‡t RJ. ‡f 1982.
32 700 12   Marsalis, Wynton, ‡d 1961- ‡t Hesitation. ‡f 1982.
33 700 12   Williams, Tony, ‡d 1945- ‡t Sister Cheryl. ‡f 1982.
34 700 12   Bricusse, Leslie. ‡t Who can I turn to. ‡f 1982.
35 700 12   Marsalis, Wynton, ‡d 1961- ‡t Twilight. ‡f 1982.
```

Field 024 is used for the UPC code on the item.
In field 007, subfields j, k, and l are omitted because they are needed only for archival materials.

Example 26: Various sources of retirement income

```
Type:    i Bib lvl: m Source: d  Lang:   eng
Repr:      Enc lvl: I Format: n  Ctry:   mnu
Accomp:    Mod rec:  Comp:   nn LTxt:   i
Desc:    a Int lvl:  Dat tp: s  Dates: 1977,
 1 040      XXX ǂc XXX
 2 007      s ǂb z ǂd z ǂe m ǂf u ǂg z ǂh n ǂi n
 3 090      HQ1062
 4 092 0    332.02401 ǂ2 20
 5 049      XXXX
 6 245 00   Various sources of retirement income ǂh sound
recording / ǂc Career Research Associates.
 7 260      [St. Paul, Minn. : ǂb 3M Visual Products Division], ǂc
c1977.
 8 300      1 sound page : ǂb analog ; ǂc 30 x 22 cm.
 9 440  0   Retirement plans ; ǂv 8.1
10 500      For use on 3M Sound Page Player.
11 650  0   Retirement.
12 650  8   Retirement.
13 710 20   Career Research Associates.
```

Note the coding of the volume number in field 440.

MOTION PICTURES AND VIDEORECORDINGS

AACR 2 Chapter 7

Example 27: A Star is Born

```
Type:       g Bib lvl: m Source:    d Lang:   eng
Type mat: v Eng lvl: I Govt pub:    Ctry:    cau
Int lvl:  g Mod rec:    Tech:     l Leng:   176
Desc:       a Accomp:     Dat tp:     s Dates:  1987,
 1 010
 2 040       XXX ǂc XXX
 3 007       v ǂb f ǂd c ǂe b ǂf a ǂg h ǂh o ǂi s
 4 092 0     791.43653 ǂ2 20
 5 090       PN1995.9.M86
 6 049       XXXX
 7 130       Star is born (1954 : Restored version)
 8 245 12    A star is born ǂh videorecording / ǂc Warner Bros Pictures ;
screen play by Moss Hart ; produced by Sidney Luft ; directed by George
Cukor.
 9 250       Restored version.
10 260       [Burbank, CA]: ǂb Warner Home Video, ǂc [1987]
11 300       2 videocassettes (176 min.) : ǂb sd., col. ; ǂc 1/2 in.
12 511 1     Judy Garland, James Mason, Jack Carson, Charles Bickford.
13 508       Music, Harold Arlen ; lyrics, Ira Gershwin.
14 500       "Based on the Dorothy Parker, Alan Campbell, Robert Carson
screen play from a story by William A. Wellman and Robert Carson."
15 500       Originally released as motion picture in 1954.
16 538       VHS hi-fi; Dolby stereo.
17 500       Rated PG.
18 520       A classic story of fame, innocence, and destruction, as a
matinee idol (Mason) falls in love with a young girl (Garland) and
propels her to stardom.
19 650   0   Musical films.
20 650   0   Feature films.
21 650   0   Motion picture actors and actresses.
21 700 11    Hart, Moss, ǂd 1904-1961.
22 700 11    Luft, Sid.
23 700 11    Cukor, George Dewey, ǂd 1899-
24 700 11    Garland, Judy.
25 700 11    Mason, James, ǂd 1909-
26 700 11    Carson, Jack, ǂd 1910-1963.
27 700 11    Bickford, Charles, ǂd 1899-1967.
28 700 11    Arlen, Harold, ǂd 1905-1986.
29 700 11    Gershwin, Ira, ǂd 1896-
30 710 21    Warner Bros. Pictures.
31 710 21    Warner Home Video.
```

The parenthetical qualifier in field 130 is not separately subfielded. Each national and local system has its own way of handling indexed fields with parenthetical qualifiers. Make sure you know what your local system does and how to retrieve information from these fields.

In the 7XX fields for this format, the only value permitted in OCLC for the second indicator is "1."

For all examples —

* Changed from form appearing in *Cataloging of Audiovisual Materials*, 3d edition. LC authority file searched June 1992.

** Cataloging changed.

Example 28: Sound of Music 25th Anniversary Edition

```
Type:       g Bib lvl: m Source:     d Lang:    eng
Type mat: v Eng lvl: I Govt pub:     Ctry:    cau
Int lvl:   g Mod rec:    Tech:     l Leng:   175
Desc:       a Accomp:     Dat tp:   s Dates: 1990,
 1 010
 2 040       XXX ǂc XXX
 3 007       v ǂb f ǂd c ǂe b ǂf a ǂg h ǂh o ǂi s
 4 092 0     782.141 ǂ2 20
 5 090       PN1995.9.M86
 6 049       XXXX
 7 245 00    Rodgers and Hammerstein's The Sound of music ǂh
videorecording / ǂc 20th Century Fox ; directed by Robert Wise;
screenplay by Ernest Lehman.
 8 250       [Silver anniversary ed.]
 9 260       [New York, N.Y.] : ǂb CBS Fox, ǂc c1990.
10 300       2 videocassettes (175 min.) : ǂb sd., col. ; ǂc 1/2 in.
11 440    5  [The Rodgers & Hammerstein collection]
12 538       VHS.
13 500       Closed captioned for the hearing impaired.
14 511 1     Julie Andrews, Christopher Plummer, Richard Haydn, Peggy
Wood, Eleanor Parker, Charmian Carr, the Bil Baird Marionettes.
15 508       Music by Richard Rodgers, lyrics by Oscar Hammerstein II,
with additional words and music by Richard Rodgers; music supervised,
arranged, and conducted by Irwin Kostal.
16 500       Originally released as motion picture in 1965.
17 500       Based on the stage musical with music and lyrics by Richard
Rodgers and Oscar Hammerstein II, book by Howard Lindsay and Russel
Crouse which was based on the lives of the Trapp Family Singers.
18 500       Stereo sound.
19 500       Rated G.
20 520       A young girl named Maria is uncertain about her decision to
enter a religious order. While deciding what to do, she becomes the
governess of the seven Von Trapp children who live with their widowed
father, a former captain in the Austrian navy. Set in Austria just
before its takeover by the Nazis.
21 500       Feature preceded by 1990 interview with director Robert Wise
and by advertisement for titles in the CBS/Fox Rodgers & Hammerstein
collection.
22 500       1829.
23 650  0    Musical films.
24 610 20    Trapp Family Singers.
25 650  0    Video recordings for the hearing impaired.
* 26 700 11  Wise, Robert, ǂd 1914-
```
(Continued on next page)

```
*  27  700  11   Lehman, Ernest, ǂd 1915-
   28  700  11   Andrews, Julie.
   29  700  11   Plummer, Christopher.
   30  700  11   Haydn, Richard.
*  31  700  11   Wood, Peggy, ǂd 1892-1978.
*  32  700  11   Parker, Eleanor, ǂd 1922-
   33  700  11   Carr, Charmian.
   34  700  11   Rodgers, Richard, ǂd 1902-
   35  700  11   Hammerstein, Oscar, ǂd 1895-1960.
   36  700  11   Lindsay, Howard.
*  37  700  11   Crouse, Russel, d 1893-1966.
   38  710  21   Twentieth Century-Fox Film Corporation.
   39  710  21   CBS Fox Video.
   40  710  21   Bil Baird Marionettes.
   41  740  41   The sound of music.
```

"Ctry" is coded for country of production rather than for the country named in field 260.

Field 511 generates the print constant "Cast:" The note in line 21 could be coded as field 505 with indicator "2," but this would generate a print constant "Partial contents:" that is unnecessary here.

Example 29: Cathedral

```
Type:       g Bib lvl: m Source:    d Lang:    eng
Type mat: v Eng lvl: I Govt pub:    Ctry:    enk
Int lvl: e Mod rec:    Tech:      c Leng:    060
Desc:       a Accomp:     Dat tp:    s Dates: 1985
   1 020       1556583362
   2 040       XXX ‡c XXX
   3 007       v ‡b f ‡d c ‡e b ‡f a ‡g h ‡h o ‡i u
   4 043       e-fr---
   5 090       NA5543
   6 092 0    726.641 ‡2 20
   7 049       XXXX
   8 245 0    Cathedral ‡h videorecording / ‡c Unicorn Projects ; written
and produced by Mark Olshaker and Larry Klein ; animation created and
directed by Tony White ; live action sequences by Carl Gover Associates
; directed by Tim King ; producer, Colin Leighton.
   9 260       [England? : ‡b Dorset Video], ‡c c1985.
  10 300       1 videocassette (60 min) : ‡b sd., col. ; ‡c 1/2 in.
  11 508       Music, Ian Llande, Steve Parr.
  12 500       Based on the book by David Macaulay.
  13 500       Originally produced for television in 1985.
  14 538       VHS.
  15 520       Follows, through animation, the planning and construction of
a Gothic cathedral in the imaginary French town of Beaulieu during the
thirteenth century. In live-action sequences David Macaulay and Caroline
Beny explain why and how the great cathedrals of Europe were built.
  16 650   0  Cathedrals ‡z France.
  17 650   0  Architecture, Gothic ‡z France.
  18 700 11  Olshaker, Mark, ‡d 1951-
* 19 700 11  Klein, Larry, ‡d 1929-
  20 700 11  White, Tony.
  21 700 11  King, Tim.
  22 700 11  Leighton, Colin.
  23 700 11  Llande, Ian.
  24 700 11  Parr, Steve.
  25 700 11  Beny, Caroline.
  26 700 11  Macaulay, David. ‡t Cathedral.
  27 710 21  Unicorn Projects, Inc.
  28 710 21  Carl Gover Associates.
  29 710 21  Dorset Video.
```

Field 538 does not include any print constant. We would not want one in this example.

Example 30: Frosty the Snowman

```
Type:       g Bib lvl: m Source:    d Lang:  eng
Type mat:   v Eng lvl: I Govt pub:    Ctry:   cau
Int lvl:    g Mod rec:    Tech:     a Leng:   030
Desc:       a Accomp:     Dat tp:   s Dates:  1989
```

```
   1 010
   2 040      XXX ‡c XXX
   3 007      v ‡b f ‡d c ‡e b ‡f a ‡g h ‡h o ‡i u
   4 090      PN1995.9.C5
   5 092 0    791.433 ‡2 20
   6 049      XXXX
   7 245 00   Frosty the Snowman ‡h videorecording / ‡c produced &
directed by Arthur Rankin, Jr. & Jules Bass ; writen by Romeo Muller.
   8 260      [Van Nuys, Calif.] : ‡b Family Home Entertainment ; ‡b
[exclusively distributed by MCA Distributing Corp., ‡c 1989]
   9 300      1 videocassette (30 min.) : ‡b sd., col. ; ‡c 1/2 in.
** 10 440 0    [Christmas classics series]
  11 511 1    Told and sung by Jimmy Durante ; Billy DeWolfe (Magician),
Jackie Vernon (Frosty).
  12 500      Based on the song by Steve Nelson and Jack Rollins.
  13 500      Produced for television in 1969.
  14 538      VHS.
  15 500      "Suitable for all ages."
  16 520      When Frosty the Snowman is accidently brought to life, he
must outwit the plans of the evil magician before finding safety at the
North Pole.
  17 650  0   Christmas stories.
  18 650  0   Children's films.
  19 650  0   Animated films.
  20 700 11   Rankin, Arthur.
  21 700 11   Bass, Jules.
  22 700 11   Muller, Romeo.
  23 700 11   Durante, Jimmy.
  24 700 11   DeWolfe, Billy.
  25 700 11   Vernon, Jackie.
  26 710 21   Family Home Entertainment.
```

In field 260 the subfield ‡b is repeated for the distribution statement.

The 440 should be in brackets because the information was taken from the package.

In field 511 the first indicator value "1" generates the print constant "Cast:" It isn't really necessary; indicator value "0" could have been used and no print constant would be generated.

Example 31: New York, New York

```
Type:        g  Bib lvl: m  Source:      d  Lang:    eng
Type mat:  v  Eng lvl: I  Govt pub:      Ctry:    cau
Int lvl:   g  Mod rec:    Tech:        l  Leng:    164
Desc:        a  Accomp:      Dat tp:    s  Dates:   1989
 1 010
 2 040        XXX ǂc XXX
 3 007        v ǂb f ǂd c ǂe b ǂf a ǂg h ǂh o ǂi s
 4 090        PN1995.9.M86
 5 092 0      791.436353 ǂ2 20
 6 049        XXXX
 7 245 00     New York, New York ǂh videorecording / ǂc United Artists ;
directed by Martin Scorsese ; produced by Irwin Winkler and Robert
Chartoff ; screenplay by Earl Mac Rauch and Mardik Martin ; story by
Earl Mac Rauch.
 8 250        Letterbox format.
 9 260        [Universal City, Calif.] : ǂb MGM/UA Home Video, ǂc [1989]
10 300        2 videocassettes (164 min.) : ǂb sd., col. ; ǂc 1/2 in.
11 500        Closed-captioned for the hearing impaired.
12 511 1      Liza Minnelli, Robert DeNiro, Lionel Stander, Barry Primus.
13 500        Original songs by John Kander and Fred Ebb.
14 500        "Original uncut version"--Package.
15 500        Originally produced as motion picture in 1977.
16 500        "Hi-fi, enhanced for stereo, digital video transfer"--
Package.
17 538        VHS.
18 500        Rated PG.
19 520        Musical celebrating the big band era, set in post-war
Manhattan. A jazz saxophone player (DeNiro) and an ex-WAC (Minnelli) who
dreams of singing, meet, marry, and work together, but their ambitions
and the pressures of show business do not permit a happy ending.
20 650  0     Musical films.
21 650  0     Feature films.
22 650  0     Video recordings for the hearing impaired.
* 23 650  0     Entertainers in motion pictures.
24 700 11     Scorsese, Martin.
25 700 11     Winkler, Irwin.
26 700 11     Chartoff, Robert.
27 700 11     Rauch, Earl Mac, ǂd 1949-
28 700 11     Martin, Mardik.
* 29 700 11     Minnelli, Liza.
30 700 11     DeNiro, Robert.
31 700 11     Stander, Lionel.
32 700 11     Primus, Barry.
33 700 11     Kander, John.
34 700 11     Ebb, Fred.
* 35 710 21     United Artists Corporation.
* 36 710 21     MGM/UA Home Video (Firm)
```

The edition statement is included in field 250 just as it is for books.

Example 32: Sorrowful Jones

```
Type:       g Bib lvl: m Source:    d Lang:   eng
Type mat: v Eng lvl: I Govt pub:    Ctry:   cau
Int lvl:  g Mod rec:    Tech:     l Leng:   088
Desc:     a Accomp:    Dat tp:    s Dates:  1988
 1 010
 2 040       XXX ‡c XXX
 3 007       v ‡b f ‡d b ‡e b ‡f a ‡g h ‡h o ‡i m
 4 090       PN1995.9.C55
 5 092 0     791.43617 ‡2 20
 6 049       XXXX
 7 245 00  Damon Runyon's Sorrowful Jones ‡h videorecording / ‡c a
Paramount Picture ; produced by Robert L. Welch ; directed by Sidney
Lanfield ; screenplay by Melville Shavelson, Edward Hartmann, and Jack
Rose.
 8 260       [Universal City, Calif.] : ‡b MCA Home Video, ‡c [1988]
 9 300       1 videocassette (88 min) : ‡b sd., b&w ; ‡c 1/2 in.
10 511 1    Bob Hope, Lucille Ball, William Demarest, Bruce Cabot, Mary
Jane Saunders.
11 511 3    Walter Winchell.
12 500       Music score, Robert Emmett Dolan.
13 500       Adapted from a story by Damon Runyon and a screenplay by
William R. Lipman, Sam Hellman, and Gladys Lehman.
14 500       Originally produced as motion picture in 1949.
15 538       VHS.
16 520       A penny-pinching Broadway bookie, Sorrowful Jones (Hope),
inherits a five-year-old girl on a bet. Big Steve (Cabot) is a bad guy
with a horse in the big race. Gladys O'Neill (Ball) is a night club
singer friendly with both Hope and Cabot.
17 650  0   Feature films.
18 650  0   Comedy films.
19 700 11   Welch, Robert L.
20 700 11   Lanfield, Sidney, ‡d 1898-1972.
* 21 700 11   Shavelson, Melville, d 1917-
22 700 11   Hartmann, Edward.
23 700 11   Rose, Jack.
24 700 11   Hope, Bob, ‡d 1903-
25 700 11   Ball, Lucille, ‡d 1911-1989.
26 700 11   Demarest, William.
27 700 11   Saunders, Mary Jane.
* 28 700 11   Winchell, Walter, d 1897-1972.
29 700 11   Dolan, Robert Emmett.
30 700 11   Runyon, Damon, ‡d 1880-1946.
* 31 710 21   Paramount Pictures, Inc.
32 710 21   MCA Home Video.
33 740 01   Sorrowful Jones.
```

The second field 511 has a first indicator value "3" to generate a print constant for narrator. This indicator will be made obsolete with format integration.

Example 33: From Page to Screen

```
Type:        g Bib lvl: m Source:    d Lang:    eng
Type mat:  v Eng lvl: I Govt pub:    Ctry:    ctu
Int lvl:   e Mod rec:    Tech:     l Leng:    026
Desc:      a Accomp:    Dat tp:   s Dates: 1981
 1 010
 2 040        XXX ǂb XXX
 3 007        v ǂb f ǂd c ǂe b ǂf a ǂg h ǂh o ǂi u
 4 090        LB1044
 5 092 0      791.4
 6 049        XXXX
 7 245 00     From page to screen ǂh videorecording / ǂc Weston Woods ;
Morton Schindel.
 8 260        [Weston, Ct.] : ǂb Weston Woods, ǂc [1981]
 9 300        1 videocassette (26 min.) : ǂb sd., col. ; ǂc 1/2 in.
10 538        VHS.
11 520        Morton Schindel recounts the history of Weston Woods
Studios, and shows how they adapt children's books to filmstrips and
movies, including writing music, recording narration, and adapting and/
or animating artwork.
12 610 20     Weston Woods Studios.
13 650  0     Motion pictures ǂx Production and direction.
14 650  0     Animated films.
15 700 11     Schindel, Morton.
16 710 21     Weston Woods Studios.
```

Example 34: Ciao, Italia

```
Type:       g Bib lvl: m Source:    d Lang:   eng
Type mat: v Eng lvl: I Govt pub:    Ctry:    it
Int lvl:  g Mod rec:   Tech:      l Leng:    100
Desc:       a Accomp:    Dat tp:    s Dates: 1988
   1 010
   2 040       XXX ǂc XXX
   3 007       v ǂb f ǂd c ǂe b ǂf a ǂg h ǂh o ǂi s
   4 092 0     781.63 ǂ2 20
   5 090       M1630.18
   6 049       XXXX
   7 100 0     Madonna, ǂd 1957-
** 8 245 10    Ciao, Italia ǂh videorecording : ǂb live from Italy / ǂc
Madonna ; produced by Ricardo Mario ; Corato Network for RAI,
Radiotelevisione Italiana ; director Egbert Van Hees.
   9 260       [Burbank, Calif. : ǂb Warner Reprise Video, ǂc 1988]
  10 300       1 videocassette (100 min.) : ǂb sd., col. ; ǂc 1/2 in.
  11 500       Concert performance.
  12 500       Songs written and performed by Madonna, with vocal and
instrumental accompaniment.
  13 508       Musical director, Pat Leonard ; concert directed and staged
by Jeffrey Hornaday.
  14 500       Dolby stereo.
  15 538       VHS format.
  16 505 0     Open your heart -- Lucky star -- True blue -- Papa don't
preach -- White heat -- Causing a commotion -- The look of love --
Medley: Dress you up, Material girl, Like a virgin -- Where's the party
-- Live to tell -- Into the groove -- La isla bonita -- Who's that girl
-- Holiday.
  17 650  0    Music videos.
  18 650  0    Popular music ǂy 1981-
  19 650  0    Rock music ǂy 1981-
  20 700 11    Mario, Ricardo.
  21 700 11    Van Hees, Egbert.
  22 700 11    Leonard, Pat.
  23 700 11    Hornaday, Jeffrey.
  24 710 21    Corato Network.
 *25 710 21    Radiotelevisione Italiana.
  26 710 21    Warner Reprise Video.
  27 700 02    Madonna, $d 1957- ǂt Open your heart (Videorecording). ǂf
1988.
  28 700 02    Madonna, $d 1957- ǂt Lucky star (Videorecording). ǂf 1988.
  29 700 02    Madonna, $d 1957- ǂt True blue (Videorecording). ǂf 1988.
  30 700 02    Madonna, $d 1957- ǂt Papa don't preach (Videorecording). ǂf
1988.
  31 700 02    Madonna, $d 1957- ǂt White heat (Videorecording). ǂf 1988.
  32 700 02    Madonna, $d 1957- ǂt Causing a commotion (Videorecording).
ǂf 1988.
  33 700 02    Madonna, $d 1957- ǂt Look of love (Videorecording). ǂf 1988.
  34 700 02    Madonna, $d 1957- ǂt Dress you up (Videorecording). ǂf 1988.
  35 700 02    Madonna, $d 1957- ǂt Material girl (Videorecording). ǂf
1988.
```

(Continued on next page)

```
36 700 02   Madonna, $d 1957- ‡t Like a virgin (Videorecording). ‡f
1988.
37 700 02   Madonna, $d 1957- ‡t Where's the party (Videorecording). ‡f
1988.
38 700 02   Madonna, $d 1957- ‡t Live to tell (Videorecording). ‡f 1988.
39 700 02   Madonna, $d 1957- ‡t Into the groove (Videorecording). ‡f
1988.
40 700 02   Madonna, $d 1957- ‡t Isla bonita (Videorecording). ‡f 1988.
41 700 02   Madonna, $d 1957- ‡t Who's that girl (Videorecording). ‡f
1988.
42 700 02   Madonna, $d 1957- ‡t Holiday (Videorecording). ‡f 1988.
```

Notice that the fixed field value "Ctry" is coded for country of production, not country of publication.

The term "videorecording" in each uniform title in the added entries is a qualifier, not a general material designation. It is used to distinguish this music video from a standard sound recording. There is not a separate subfield code for this qualifier.

Example 35A: Singin' in the Rain VHS

```
Type:       g Bib lvl: m Source:    d Lang:   eng
Type mat: v Eng lvl: I Govt pub:    Ctry:   cau
Int lvl:  g Mod rec:    Tech:    l Leng:  103
Desc:      a Accomp:     Dat tp:   s Dates: 1983
 1 010
 2 040      XXX ‡c XXX
 3 007      v ‡b f ‡d c ‡e b ‡f a ‡g h ‡h o ‡i u
 4 092 0    791.43653 ‡2 20
 5 090      PN1995.M86
 6 049      XXXX
 7 245 00   Singin' in the rain ‡h videorecording / ‡c Metro Goldwyn
Mayer ; produced by Arthur Freed ; directed by Gene Kelly and Stanley
Donen ; story and screen play by Adolph Green and Betty Comden.
 8 260      [New York, NY] : ‡b MGM/UA Home Video, ‡c [1983]
 9 300      1 videocassette (103 min.) : ‡b sd., col. ; ‡c 1/2 in.
10 511 1    Gene Kelly, Debbie Reynolds, Donald O'Connor, Jean Hagen,
Millard Mitchell, Cyd Charisse.
11 508      Lyrics by Arthur Freed ; music by Nacio Herb Brown.
12 500      Originally released as motion picture in 1952.
13 538      VHS.
14 520      Musical comedy parody of Hollywood's transition to "talking
pictures" in the 1920s.
15 650 0    Musical films.
16 650 0    Feature films.
17 650 0    Sound motion pictures ‡x History.
18 700 11   Freed, Arthur, ‡d 1894-1973.
19 700 11   Kelly, Gene, ‡d 1912-
20 700 11   Donen, Stanley.
21 700 11   Green, Adolph.
22 700 11   Comden, Betty.
23 700 11   Reynolds, Debbie.
24 700 11   O'Connor, Donald, ‡d 1925-
25 700 11   Hagen, Jean, ‡d 1924-1977.
26 700 11   Mitchell, Millard.
27 700 11   Charisse, Cyd.
28 700 11   Brown, Nacio Herb, ‡d 1896-
29 710 21   Metro-Goldwyn-Mayer.
* 30 710 21   MGM/UA Home Video (Firm)
```

Field 508 is used for people involved in the production of a work, field 511 is for members of the cast.

Example 35B: Singin' in the Rain CLV

```
Type:        g Bib lvl: m Source:     d Lang:    eng
Type mat:  v Eng lvl: I Govt pub:      Ctry:   cau
Int lvl:   g Mod rec:    Tech:      l Leng:   103
Desc:        a Accomp:      Dat tp:   s Dates: 1983
 1 010
 2 020      0559400722
 3 040      XXX ‡c XXX
 4 007      v ‡b d ‡d c ‡e g ‡f a ‡g i ‡h z ‡i u
 5 092  0   791.43653 ‡2 20
 6 090      PN1995.M86
 7 049      XXXX
 8 245 00   Singin' in the rain ‡h videorecording / ‡c Metro Goldwyn
Mayer ; produced by Arthur Freed ; directed by Gene Kelly and Stanley
Donen ; story and screen play by Adolph Green and Betty Comden.
 9 260      [Santa Monica, CA : ‡b Distributed by the Voyager Co., ‡c
1990]
10 300      1 videodisc (103 min.) : ‡b sd., col. ; ‡c 12 in.
11 440   4  The Criterion Collection ; ‡v 52A
12 511 1    Gene Kelly, Debbie Reynolds, Donald O'Connor, Jean Hagen,
Millard Mitchell, Cyd Charisse.
13 508      Lyrics by Arthur Freed ; music by Nacio Herb Brown.
14 500      Originally released as motion picture in 1952.
15 538      Extended play (CLV).
16 500      Rated G.
17 520      Musical comedy parody of Hollywood's transition to "talking
pictures" in the 1920s.
18 500      "CC1210L."
19 650   0  Musical films.
20 650   0  Feature films.
21 650   0  Sound motion pictures ‡x History.
22 700 11   Freed, Arthur, ‡d 1894-1973.
23 700 11   Kelly, Gene, ‡d 1912-
24 700 11   Donen, Stanley.
25 700 11   Green, Adolph.
26 700 11   Comden, Betty.
27 700 11   Reynolds, Debbie.
28 700 11   O'Connor, Donald, ‡d 1925-
29 700 11   Hagen, Jean, ‡d 1924-1977.
30 700 11   Mitchell, Millard.
31 700 11   Charisse, Cyd.
31 710 21   Metro-Goldwyn-Mayer.
32 710 21   Voyager Company.
```

The ISBN is recorded in field 020.

Example 35C: Singin' in the Rain CAV

```
Type:       g Bib lvl: m Source:    d Lang:   eng
Type mat: v Eng lvl: I Govt pub:   Ctry:   cau
Int lvl:  g Mod rec:   Tech:     l Leng:
Desc:       a Accomp:    Dat tp:   s Dates: 1983
 1 010
 2 020      0931393981
 3 040      XXX ‡c XXX
 4 007      v ‡b d ‡d c ‡e g ‡f a ‡g i ‡h z ‡i u
 5 092 0    791.43653 ‡2 20
 6 090      PN1995.M86
 7 049      XXXX
 8 245 00   Singin' in the rain ‡h videorecording / ‡c Metro Goldwyn
Mayer ; produced by Arthur Freed ; directed by Gene Kelly and Stanley
Donen ; story and screen play by Adolph Green and Betty Comden.
 9 260      [Santa Monica, CA : ‡b Distributed by the Voyager Co., ‡c
1988]
10 300      2 videodiscs : ‡b sd., col. ; ‡c 12 in.
** 11 440   4  The Criterion collection ; ‡v 52
12 511 1    Gene Kelly, Debbie Reynolds, Donald O'Connor, Jean Hagen,
Millard Mitchell, Cyd Charisse.
13 508      Lyrics by Arthur Freed ; music by Nacio Herb Brown.
14 500      Originally released as motion picture in 1952.
15 538      Full feature format (CAV).
16 520      Musical comedy parody of Hollywood's transition to "talking
pictures" in the 1920s.
17 500      Audio essay by Ronald Haver is on the second audio track.
18 500      Following the film are original film versions of the songs
Singin' in the rain (Cliff Edwards), Beautiful girl (Bing Crosby), and
You were meant for me (Charles King and Anita Page).  Also included are
an early demonstration of talking movies, and an outtake from the film.
19 500      "CC1152L."
20 650   0  Musical films.
21 650   0  Feature films.
22 650   0  Sound motion pictures ‡x History.
23 700  11  Freed, Arthur, ‡d 1894-1973.
24 700  11  Kelly, Gene, ‡d 1912-
25 700  11  Donen, Stanley.
26 700  11  Green, Adolph.
27 700  11  Comden, Betty.
28 700  11  Reynolds, Debbie.
29 700  11  O'Connor, Donald, ‡d 1925-
30 700  11  Hagen, Jean, ‡d 1924-1977.
31 700  11  Mitchell, Millard.
32 700  11  Charisse, Cyd.
33 710  21  Metro-Goldwyn-Mayer.
34 710  21  Voyager Company.
```

Example 36A: Tummy Trouble

```
Type:       g Bib lvl: m Source:     d Lang:    eng
Type mat: v Eng lvl: I Govt pub:    Ctry:    cau
Int lvl:  g Mod rec:    Tech:     l Leng:    008
Desc:       a Accomp:    Dat tp:    s Dates: 1987,
  1 010
  2 020       1558909095
  3 040       XXX ǂc XXX
  4 007       v ǂb f ǂd c ǂe b ǂf a ǂg h ǂh o ǂi s
  5 092 0     791.43617 ǂ2 20
  6 090       PN1995.9.C55
  7 049       XXXX
  8 245 00    Tummy trouble ǂh videorecording / ǂc Walt Disney Pictures ;
[presented by] Steven Spielberg ; Amblin Entertainment ; produced by Don
Hahn ; animation directed by Rob Minkhoff ; live action directed by
Frank Marshall.
  9 260       [Burbank, CA] : ǂb Walt Disney Home Video ; ǂb distributed
by Buena Vista Pictures, ǂc c1990.
 10 300       on 1 videocassette (8 min.) : ǂb sd., col. ; ǂc 1/2 in.
 11 500       "A Maroon cartoon"
 12 500       Closed-captioned for the hearing impaired.
 13 538       VHS, stereo.
 14 520       "When Baby Herman swallows a rattle, it's Roger Rabbit who's
all shook up as these two toons take over a hospital and stir up a
little medical mayhem"--Container.
 15 501       With: Honey, I shrunk the kids.
 16 650   0   Animated films.
 17 600 10    Rabbit, Roger.
 18 600 00    Baby Herman.
 19 700 11    Spielberg, Steven, ǂd 1947-
 20 700 11    Hahn, Don.
 21 700 11    Minkhoff, Rob.
 22 700 11    Marshall, Frank.
 23 710 21    Walt Disney Pictures.
 24 710 21    Amblin Entertainment (Firm)
* 25 710 21    Walt Disney Home Video (Firm)
 26 710 21    Buena Vista Pictures.
```

Field 501 is the last note. Notes are put in order by AACR 2 rule number, not by the 5XX number.

Example 36B: Honey, I Shrunk the Kids

```
Type:        g Bib lvl: m Source:    d Lang:   eng
Type mat: v Eng lvl: I Govt pub:    Ctry:   cau
Int lvl:  g Mod rec:    Tech:     l Leng:   101
Desc:       a Accomp:    Dat tp:  s Dates:  1987,
```

```
 1 010
 2 020      1558909095
 3 040      XXX ‡c XXX
 4 007      v ‡b f ‡d c ‡e b ‡f a ‡g h ‡h o ‡i s
 5 092 0    791.43617 ‡2 20
 6 090      PN1995.9.C55
 7 049      XXXX
 8 245 00   Honey, I shrunk the kids ‡h videorecording / ‡c Walt Disney
Pictures ; Silver Screen Partners III ; produced by Penney Finkelman Cox
; directed by Joe Johnston.
 9 260      [Burbank, CA] : ‡b Walt Disney Home Video ; ‡b [distributed
by Buena Vista Home Video], ‡c c1990.
10 300      1 videocassette (101 min.) : ‡b sd., col. ; ‡c 1/2 in.
11 500      Closed-captioned for the hearing impaired.
12 508      Story, Stuart Gordon, Brian Yuzna, Ed Naha ; screenplay, Ed
Naha, Tom Schulman.
13 500      Originally produced as motion picture in 1989.
14 538      VHS, stereo.
15 500      Rated PG.
16 520      An absent-minded inventor (Rick Moranis) working on a
shrinking machine accidentally shrinks his kids down to 1/4 inch in
height! When they are tossed out with the trash they have to make their
way home through a backyard that has become a jungle.
17 500      Preceded by a preview of the movie Dick Tracy.
18 501      With: Tummy trouble.
19 650  0   Comedy films.
20 650  0   Science fiction films.
21 650  0   Video recordings for the hearing impaired.
22 700 11   Cox, Penney Finkelman.
23 700 11   Johnston, Joe.
24 700 11   Gordon, Stuart.
25 700 11   Yuzna, Brian.
26 700 11   Naha, Ed.
27 700 11   Schulman, Tom.
28 700 11   Moranis, Rick.
29 710 21   Walt Disney Pictures.
30 710 21   Silver Screen Partners III.
* 31 710 21 Walt Disney Home Video (Firm)
* 32 710 21 Buena Vista Home Video (Firm)
```

Field 508 generates the print constant "Credits:"

Example 37: Mitosis

```
Type:       g Bib lvl: m Source:    d Lang:   eng
Type mat: m Eng lvl: I Govt pub:    Ctry:    ilu
Int lvl:  f Mod rec:    Tech:     z Leng:    004
Desc:       a Accomp:    Dat tp:   s Dates: 1967,
 1 040      XXX ǂc XXX
 2 007      m ǂb c ǂd c ǂe a ǂf  ǂg  ǂh b
 3 090      QH605.2
 4 092 0    574.87623 ǂ2 19
 5 049      XXXX
 6 245 00   Mitosis ǂh motion picture / ǂc produced by the
Biological Sciences Curriculum Study.
 7 260      Northbrook, Ill. : ǂb Hubbard, ǂc c1967.
 8 300      1 film loop (4 min.) : ǂb si., col. ; ǂc super 8 mm. +
ǂe 1 self-instruction inquiry guide.
 9 440  2   A BSCS single topic inquiry film
10 520      Uses time-lapse photography to show the process of
mitosis.
11 650  0   Mitosis.
12 650  0   Cell division.
13 650  8   Cells.
14 650  8   Reproduction.
15 710 21   Biological Sciences Curriculum Study.
16 710 21   Hubbard Scientific Company.
```

"Tech" is coded "z", i.e., "other", for time-lapse photography.

Example 38: Trisecting a Line

```
Type:       g Bib lvl: m Source:    d Lang:    eng
Type mat:  m Eng lvl: I Govt pub:    Ctry:    xxu
Int lvl:   d Mod rec:    Tech:     l Leng:    004
Desc:      a Accomp:     Dat tp:   s Dates:  1969,
 1 040      XXX ǂc XXX
 2 007      m ǂb c ǂd c ǂe a ǂf   ǂg   ǂh b
 3 090      QA459
 4 092  0   516.2076 ǂ2 19
 5 049      XXXX
 6 245      Trisecting a line with triangles ǂh motion picture
 7 260      [United States] : ǂb Heath, ǂc c1969.
 8 300      1 film cartridge (ca. 4 min.) : ǂb sd., col. ; ǂc
super 8 mm.
 9 440  0   Basic drafting techniques ; ǂv 015/24
10 500      Title on cartridge and container: Trisecting a
straight line with triangles.
11 508      Designed by Charles Coiro ; copyright by the Walden
Film Corporation.
12 500      For use on Kodak Supermatic Projector.
13 520      Shows how to trisect a straight line using a 30/60/90
triangle and a T-square.
14 650  0   Geometry ǂx Problems, exercises, etc.
15 650  8   Geometry ǂx Problems, exercises, etc.
16 700 11   Coiro, Charles.
17 710 21   Walden Film Corporation.
18 740  0   Trisecting a straight line with triangles.
```

The fixed field "Int lvl" (Intellectual level) is coded "d," assuming senior high is the highest level at which this item might be used. It could be coded "f" for specialized.

Example 39: News Images

```
Type:       g Bib lvl: m Source:    d Lang:    eng
Type mat: v Eng lvl: I Govt pub:    Ctry:    mnu
Int lvl:  f Mod rec:    Tech:     l Leng:    015
Desc:       a Accomp:    Dat tp:   s Dates: 1978
   1 040      XXX ‡c XXX
   2 007      v ‡b f ‡d c ‡e c ‡f a ‡g h ‡h r
   3 043      n-us-mn
   4 090      PN4888.T4
   5 092 0    070.4 ‡2 19
   6 049      XXXX
   7 245 00   News images, television and print ‡h videorecording :
‡b television news and photojournalism in the Twin Cities / ‡c
produced by Walker Art Center ; director, Charles Helm ; producer
and script writer, Maud Lavin.
   8 260      Minneapolis : ‡b The Center, ‡c c1978.
   9 300      1 videocassette (15 min.) : ‡b sd., col. ; ‡c 1/2 in.
  10 511 3    Dave Moore.
  11 500      Produced with the assistance of WCCO-TV.
  12 538      VHS.
  13 520      Describes and compares television journalism and press
photography using examples of Minneapolis and St. Paul news items.
  14 650  0   Broadcast journalism.
* 15 650  0   Photojournalism.
  16 650  0   Television broadcasting of news.
  17 650  8   Television broadcasting.
  18 650  8   Photography, Journalistic.
* 19 700 11   Moore, Dave, ‡d 1924-
  20 700 11   Helm, Charles.
  21 700 11   Lavin, Maud.
  22 710 21   Walker Art Center.
  23 710 21   WCCO-TV (Television station : Minneapolis, Minn.)
  24 740 01   Television and print.
  25 740 01   Television news and photojournalism in the Twin
Cities.
  26 740 01   News images.
```

Here "Int lvl" is coded "f" for specialized. The value "g" for general is reserved for fictional works.

Example 40: 100 Years of Brewing

```
Type:       g Bib lvl: m Source:    d Lang:   eng
Type mat: v Eng lvl: I Govt pub:    Ctry:   mnu
Int lvl:  g Mod rec:    Tech:     l Leng:   030
Desc:       a Accomp:     Dat tp:   s Dates: 1971
 1 040     XXX ‡c XXX
 2 007     v ‡b f ‡d b ‡e c ‡f a ‡g h ‡h r
 3 043     n-us-mn
 4 045     w6x6
 5 090     HD9397.U53
 6 092 0   663.309776 ‡2 19
 7 049     XXXX
 8 245 00  100 years of brewing ‡h videorecording / ‡c written
and produced by Joyce Peterson and Rod Terbeest ; directed by Rod
Terbeest ; produced in association with the Regional Television
Production Center, Mankato State College.
 9 260     Mankato, Minn. : ‡b The Center, ‡c [1971]
10 300     1 videocassette (30 min.) : ‡b sd., b&w ; ‡c 3/4 in.
11 508     Narrator, Curt Crandall ; music, Lowell Schreyer,
Michael Scullin ; project adviser, William McGinley.
12 538     U-matic.
13 520     A documentary of the history of the brewing industry
in Mankato, Minnesota.
14 650   0 Brewing industry ‡z Minnesota.
15 650   8 Beverages.
16 700 11  Peterson, Joyce.
17 700 11  Terbeest, Rod.
18 700 11  Crandall, Curt.
19 700 11  McGinley, William A., ‡d 1943-
20 700 11  Schreyer, Lowell.
21 700 11  Scullin, Michael.
22 710 21  Mankato State College. ‡b Regional Television
Production Center.
23 740 01  One hundred years of brewing.
```

Field 043 is coded for the geographic aspect, field 045 for the time period involved.

Example 41: Out of the Closet

```
Type:       g Bib lvl: m Source:    d Lang:    eng
Type mat: v Eng lvl: I Govt pub:   Ctry:    mnu
Int lvl:  g Mod rec:   Tech:     l Leng:    030
Desc:       a Accomp:    Dat tp:    s Dates: 1977
  1 040      XXX ‡c XXX
  2 007      v ‡b f ‡d c ‡e b ‡f a ‡g h ‡h o
  3 090      HQ76.25
  4 092 0    306.7 ‡2 19
  5 049      XXXX
  6 245 00   Out of the closet ‡h videorecording / ‡c produced and
written by Jim Hayden.
  7 260      ‡c [1977]
  8 300      1 videocassette (30 min.) ; ‡b sd., col. ; ‡c 1/2 in.
  9 490 1    Moore on Sunday
 10 500      Title from narration.
 11 500      A presentation of the Public Affairs Unit, WCCO
Television News.
 12 500      Broadcast on WCCO-TV Oct. 23, 1977; taped with
permission.
 13 538      VHS-SP.
 14 520      Commentary on the oppression of gays, role of Anita
Bryant, and Minneapolis reaction.
 15 650  0   Homosexuality.
 16 650  8   Gay men.
 17 650  8   Gay women.
 18 650  8   Homosexuality.
*19 700 11   Moore, Dave, ‡d 1924-
 20 700 11   Bryant, Anita.
 21 710 21   WCCO-TV (Television station : Minneapolis, Minn.)
 22 830  0   Moore on Sunday (Television program)
```

Example 42: Power, Politics & Current Issues in Rehabilitation

```
Type:       g Bib lvl: m Source:    d Lang:    eng
Type mat: v Eng lvl: I Govt pub:    Ctry:    mnu
Int lvl:  f Mod rec:   Tech:     l Leng:    060
Desc:       a Accomp:     Dat tp:  s Dates: 1977
 1 040      XXX ǂc XXX
 2 007      v ǂb f ǂd b ǂe d ǂf a ǂg h ǂh o
 3 090      HD7255
 4 092  0   362.4 ǂ2 19
 5 049      XXXX
 6 245 00   Power, politics & current issues in rehabilitation ǂh
videorecording : ǂb workshop / ǂc presented by Rehabilitation
Counseling Department, Mankato State University.
 7 260      ǂc [1977]
 8 300      1 videoreel (60 min.) : ǂb sd., b&w ; ǂc 1/2 in.
 9 500      Workshop director, Ward Thayer; project director
Richard Ugland; dept. chair, Robert Hopper.
10 520      Senator Hubert H. Humphrey speaks at a workshop held
July 6, 1977, at Mankato State University, on the use of politics
and the applications of power in advancing the program,
objectives, and goals of handicapped and disabled persons.
11 650  0   Rehabilitation.
12 650  8   Physically handicapped ǂx Rehabilitation.
13 700 11   Humphrey, Hubert H. ǂq (Hubert Horatio), ǂd 1911-1978.
14 700 11   Thayer, Ward.
15 700 11   Ugland, Richard.
16 700 11   Hopper, Robert.
17 710 21   Mankato State University. ǂb Rehabilitation Counseling
Department.
18 740 01   Power, politics, and current issues in rehabilitation.
```

This unpublished item has only subfield ǂc in field 260.

Example 43: The Age of Steam

```
Type:       g Bib lvl: m Source:    d Lang:    eng
Type mat: v Eng lvl: I Govt pub:    Ctry:    inu
Int lvl:  f Mod rec:   Tech:      l Leng:    030
Desc:       a Accomp:    Dat tp:    s Dates: 1968
 1 040      XXX ǂc XXX
 2 007      v ǂb f ǂd b ǂe c ǂf a ǂg h ǂh r
 3 090      TJ615
 4 092 0    385.09 ǂ2 19
 5 049      XXXX
 6 100 1    McGinley, William A., ǂd 1943-
 7 245 14   The age of steam ǂh videorecording / ǂc written,
produced, and directed by William A. McGinley ; special assistance
by Thomas E. Harmening and George H. Collins.
 8 260      ǂc 1968.
 9 300      1 videocassette (30 min.) : ǂb sd., b&w ; ǂc 3/4 in.
10 500      Produced in association with Indiana University
Department of Radio and Television.
11 538      U-matic.
12 502      Thesis (M.A.)--Indiana University, 1968.
13 520      Brief historical study of the steam locomotive from
its inception to its replacement by the diesel.
14 650   0  Locomotives.
15 650   0  Steam engineering.
16 650   8  Locomotives.
17 650   8  Steam engineering.
18 700 11   Harmening, Thomas E.
19 700 11   Collins, George H.
20 710 21   Indiana University. ǂb Dept. of Radio and Television.
```

This is an unpublished item. For audiovisual materials the fixed field "Ctry" is for country of *production*, not of *publication*, so it is coded as shown.

GRAPHIC MATERIALS

AACR 2 Chapter 8

Example 44: Selecting Leisure Activities

```
Type:       g Bib lvl: m Source:   d Lang:   eng
Type mat: f Enc lvl: I Govt pub:   Ctry:   cau
Int lvl:  f Mod rec:   Tech:     n Leng:   nnn
Desc:       a Accomp:   Dat tp:   s Dates: 1979,
  1 040     XXX ǂc XXX
  2 007     g ǂb o ǂd c ǂe j ǂf b ǂg f ǂh f ǂi
  3 090     BJ1498
  4 092 0   790.013 ǂ2 20
  5 049     XXXX
  6 245 00  Selecting leisure activities ǂh filmstrip / ǂc
produced by Multi-Media Productions, Inc. ; written and
photographed by John Loughary, Theresa Ripley, and Vanesa Tsang.
  7 260     Stanford, CA : ǂb Multi-Media Productions, ǂc c1979.
  8 300     1 filmstrip (61 fr.) : ǂb col. ; ǂc 35 mm. + ǂe 1
sound cassette (20 min. : analog) + 1 program script + 1 teacher's
manual.
  9 520     Discusses 15 satisfactions of leisure activities as
well as conditions to be considered such as time, costs, physical
needs, skills, and aptitude.
 10 650  0  Leisure.
 11 650  0  Recreation.
 12 650  0  Time allocation.
 13 650  8  Leisure.
 14 650  8  Recreation.
 15 650  8  Hobbies.
*16 700 11  Loughary, John William, ǂd 1930-
*17 700 11  Ripley, Theresa M.
 18 700 11  Tsang, Vanesa.
*19 710 21  Multi-Media Productions.
```

The fixed field "Accomp" is used primarily for archival cataloging. It is optional, so it will be left blank in these examples. All type "g" materials require field 007.

Field 007 subfield ǂa is coded "g" for all projected graphics.

For all examples —

* Changed from form appearing in *Cataloging of Audiovisual Materials*, 3d edition. LC authority file searched June 1992.

** Cataloging changed.

Example 45A: Word Processing

```
Type:        g Bib lvl: m Source:    d Lang:   eng
Type mat: f Enc lvl: I Govt pub:    Ctry:   mdu
Int lvl:  f Mod rec:   Tech:    n Leng:   nnn
Desc:        a Accomp:    Dat tp:   s Dates: 1978,
  1 040       XXX ǂc XXX
  2 007       g ǂb o ǂd c ǂe j ǂf b ǂg f ǂh f ǂi
  3 090       HF5548.115
  4 092 0     652.5 ǂ2 20
  5 049       XXXX
  6 245 00    Word processing ǂh filmstrip / ǂc an audiovisual
production of the Robert J. Brady Co.
  7 260       Bowie, MD : ǂb Brady, ǂc c1978.
  8 300       6 filmstrips : ǂb col. ; ǂc 35 mm. + ǂe 6 sound
cassettes + 1 instructional guide in container 33 x 33 x 8 cm.
  9 520       Designed to introduce word processing systems to
students in business programs or to office workers in traditional
setting.
10 505 0     module 1. Introducing word processing (95 fr.) --
module 2. Word processing organizations (80 fr.) -- module 3. Work
flow (106 fr.) -- module 4. Careers (80 fr.) -- module 5.
Equipment orientation (101 fr.) -- module 6. Office of the future
(79 fr.).
11 650  0    Word processing.
12 650  8    Word processing.
13 710 21    Robert J. Brady Company.
```

Fixed field "Tech" (technique) is coded "n" unless the item is a motion picture or a videorecording. In field 007, subfield ǂa is coded "j" for safety film for these filmstrips.

Example 45B: Careers

```
Type:       g Bib lvl: m Source:    d Lang:   eng
Type mat: f Enc lvl: I Govt pub:    Ctry:   mdu
Int lvl:  f Mod rec:   Tech:      n Leng:   nnn
Desc:       a Accomp:     Dat tp:   s Dates: 1978,
 1 040      XXX ǂc XXX
 2 007      g ǂb o ǂd c ǂe j ǂf b ǂg f ǂh f ǂi
 3 090      HF5548
 4 092 0    652.54023 ǂ2 20
 5 049      XXXX
 6 245 00   Careers ǂh filmstrip / ǂc produced by Robert J. Brady
Co.
 7 260      Bowie, Md. : ǂb Brady, ǂc c1978.
 8 300      1 filmstrip (80 fr.) : ǂb col. ; ǂc 35 mm. + ǂe 1
sound cassette + 1 manual.
 9 440  0   Word processing ; ǂv module 4
10 500      Title on manual: Career paths.
11 520      Discusses career possibilities using word processing
systems and explains tasks and levels of responsibility in a word
processing center and in an administrative office.
12 650  0   Career education.
13 650  0   Word processing ǂx Vocational guidance.
14 650  8   Occupations.
15 650  8   Word processing ǂx Study and teaching.
16 710 21   Robert J. Brady Company.
17 740 01   Career paths.
```

Fixed field "Leng" (length) now is used only for motion pictures and videorecordings.

Example 46: Surveillance

```
Type:       g Bib lvl: m Source:    d Lang:   eng
Type mat: s Enc lvl: I Govt pub:    Ctry:   ilu
Int lvl:  f Mod rec:   Tech:      n Leng:   nnn
Desc:       a Accomp:     Dat tp:  s Dates: 1976,
 1 040       XXX ǂc XXX
 2 007       g ǂb s ǂd c ǂe j ǂf b ǂg f ǂh j ǂi c
 3 090       HV8080.P2
 4 092 0     363.232 ǂ2 20
 5 049       XXXX
 6 245 00    Surveillance ǂh slide / ǂc produced for United
Learning for Police Science Services.
 7 260       Niles, Ill. : ǂb United Learning, ǂc c1976.
 8 300       80 slides : ǂb col. + ǂe 1 sound cassette + 1 manual +
1 set study notes + 1 set quiz questions.
 9 500       Title from container. Title on title frame of
filmstrip: Make the case with surveillance.
10 520       Includes instruction on foot, vehicular, and fixed
surveillance, as well as information on avoiding detection,
working with non-surveillance officers, equipment, and reporting.
Safety precautions are emphasized.
11 650   0   Police patrol ǂx Surveillance operations.
12 650   0   Criminal investigation.
13 650   8   Criminal investigation.
14 650   8   Law enforcement ǂx Techniques.
15 710 21    United Learning (Firm)
16 710 21    Police Science Services, Inc.
17 740 01    Make the case with surveillance.
```

Subfield ǂe in field 300 is not repeated. The one subfield includes all accompanying material.

In field 007, subfield ǂf is coded "b" for sound on a separate item, and subfield ǂg is coded "f" for sound cassette..

Example 47: Mount Rainier

```
Type:        g Bib lvl: m Source:     d Lang:     eng
Type mat:  s Enc lvl: I Govt pub:     Ctry:     xxu
Int lvl:   e Mod rec:   Tech:       n Leng:     nnn
Desc:      a Accomp:    Dat tp:     q Dates: 1970,1979
  1 040       XXX ‡c XXX
  2 007       g ‡b s ‡d c ‡e j ‡h j ‡i c
  3 043       n-us-wa
  4 090       GB2425.W3
  5 092 0     917.97782 ‡2 20
  6 049       XXXX
  7 245 00    Mount Rainier, Wash. ‡h slide : ‡b aerial of glaciers.
  8 260       [United States] : ‡b Pana-Vue, ‡c [197-?]
  9 300       1 slide : ‡b col.
 10 500       "S 1967".
 11 651  0    Rainier, Mount (Wash.)
 12 650  0    Glaciers.
 13 651  8    Mount Rainier (Wash.)
 14 710 21    Pana-Vue (Firm)
 15 740 01    Aerial of glaciers.
```

Fixed field "Int lvl" is coded "e" for adult (non-fiction). In field 007 subfield ‡b is coded "s" for slide.

Example 48: MV 20 Film Card Sample

```
Type:        g Bib lvl: m Source:     d Lang:     eng
Type mat:  z Enc lvl: I Govt pub:     Ctry:     azu
Int lvl:   f Mod rec:   Tech:       n Leng:     nnn
Desc:      a Accomp:    Dat tp:     s Dates: 1982,
  1 040       XXX ‡c XXX
  2 007       g ‡b z ‡d c ‡e j ‡h z
  3 090       LB1043.7
  4 092 0     371.335 ‡2 20
  5 049       XXXX
  6 245 00    MV 20 film card sample.
  7 260       Tempe, Ariz. : ‡b Multi Vue, ‡c [1982]
  8 300       1 film cards (20 fr.) : ‡b col. ; ‡c 7 x 10 cm.
  9 500       Sample of "film card" made from color slides.
 10 650  0    Audio-visual materials.
 11 650  8    Audio-visual materials.
 12 710 21    Multi Vue (Firm)
```

Fixed field "type mat" is coded "z" for other. In field 007 subfield ‡b is coded "z" for other projected graphic type.

Example 49: Random Sampling

```
Type:        g Bib lvl: m Source:     d Lang:   eng
Type mat: t Enc lvl: I Govt pub:    Ctry:   cau
Int lvl:  f Mod rec:   Tech:     n Leng:   nnn
Desc:        a Accomp:      Dat tp:    s Dates: 1973,
  1 040      XXX ‡c XXX
  2 007      g ‡b t ‡d c ‡e k ‡h z ‡i c
  3 090      QA276.6
  4 092 0    519.52 ‡2 20
  5 049      XXXX
  6 245 00   Random sampling ‡h transparency
  7 260      San Jose, Calif. : ‡b Lansford Pub. Co., ‡c c1973.
  8 300      15 transparencies : ‡b col. ; ‡c 19 x 26 cm. + ‡e 1
teacher's guide.
  9 500      Guide by D. Wassenaar.
 10 520      Illustrates simple random sampling and some of its
applications.
 11 505 0    The process of random sampling -- A visual
demonstration of sampling -- Plotting the population distribution
-- Calculating population mean and standard deviation -- How to
draw a random sample -- Practical methods for drawing random
samples -- Calculating a sample mean and standard deviation -- The
sampling distribution of the means -- The normal distribution --
Confidence level estimates -- Determining required sample size --
Balancing cost versus accuracy -- The binomial distribution --
Relationship between population size and required sample size --
Political polls.
 12 500      "W340T"
 13 650   0  Sampling (Statistics)
 14 650   8  Sampling (Statistics)
* 15 700 11  Wassenaar, Dirk.
 16 710 21  Lansford Publishing Company.
```

Fixed field "Int lvl" is coded "f" for specialized. This is college-level material.

Subfield ‡b of field 007 is coded "t" for transparency. Subfield ‡i is coded "c" to indicate these are mounted in cardboard.

Example 50: Composition of the Earth

```
Type:       g Bib lvl: m Source:    d Lang:   eng
Type mat: t Enc lvl: I Govt pub:    Ctry:  mou
Int lvl:  d Mod rec:   Tech:     n Leng: nnn
Desc:       a Accomp:     Dat tp:    s Dates: 1971,
 1 040      XXX ǂc XXX
 2 007      g ǂb t ǂd c ǂe k ǂh z
 3 090      QE509
 4 092 0    551.1 ǂ2 20
 5 049      XXXX
 6 100 1    Leftwich, Virginia Powers.
 7 245 10   Composition of the earth ǂh transparency / ǂc written
by Virginia Powers Leftwich ; illustrated by Larry Weaver.
 8 260      St. Louis, Mo. : ǂb Milliken Pub. Co., ǂc c1971.
 9 300      12 transparencies : ǂb col. ; ǂc 21 x 28 cm. + ǂe 16
duplicating pages + 1 teacher's guide (12 p. ; 28 cm.)
10 440  0   Earth science series
11 500      "A Milliken full color transparency-duplicating book"-
-Cover.
12 500      Transparencies and duplicating masters are perforated
for removal.
13 651  0   Earth ǂx Internal structure.
14 651  8   Earth ǂx Internal structure.
15 700 11   Weaver, Larry.
* 16 710 21  Milliken Publishing Company.
```

In field 007 subfield ǂe is coded "k" for film other than safety film.

Example 51: Dependent Clauses

```
Type:       k Bib lvl: m Source:    d Lang:   eng
Type mat: i Enc lvl: I Govt pub:    Ctry:  mnu
Int lvl:  d Mod rec:   Tech:     n Leng: nnn
Desc:       a Accomp:     Dat tp:    q Dates: 1960,1969
 1 040      XXX ǂc XXX
 2 007      k ǂb z ǂd b ǂe o
 3 090      PE1385
 4 092 0    425 ǂ2 19
 5 049      XXXX
 6 100 1    Searles, John R.
 7 245 10   Dependent clauses / ǂc by John R. Searles.
 8 260      St. Paul, Minn. : ǂb 3M, ǂc [196-?]
 9 300      31 printed originals : ǂb b&w ; ǂc 28 x 22 cm.
10 440  0   English packet ; ǂv number 5
11 500      "Printed originals for preparing overhead projection
transparencies"--Cover.
12 650  0   English language ǂx Clauses.
13 650  8   English language ǂx Grammar.
* 14 710 21  Minnesota Mining and Manufacturing Company.
```

Type "k" material is printed graphics that are not projected. All type "k" materials require field 007. Subfield ǂb is coded "z" for other, including transparency masters.

Example 52: 50 Puzzles

```
Type:       k Bib lvl: m Source:     d Lang:    eng
Type mat: i Enc lvl: I Govt pub:     Ctry:    meu
Int lvl:  f Mod rec:   Tech:       n Leng:    nnn
Desc:       a Accomp:     Dat tp:    s Dates: 1979
 1 040      XXX ‡c XXX
 2 007      k ‡b z ‡d b ‡e o
 3 090      HF5415.4
 4 092 0    650.07 ‡2 19
 5 049      XXXX
 6 100 1    Muscatello, William R.
 7 245 10   50 puzzles for distributive education classes / ‡c
William R. Muscatello.
 8 260      Portland, Me. : ‡b J. Weston Walch, ‡c c1979.
 9 300      50 spirit masters : ‡b b&w ; ‡c 28 x 22 cm. + ‡e 1
answer key in box.
10 520      Educational puzzles for use in junior high through
vocational school.
11 650   0  Distributive education.
12 650   0  Business education.
13 650   8  Business education.
* 14 710 01  J. Weston Walch, Publisher.
15 740 01   Fifty puzzles for distributive education classes.
```

These spirit masters don't quite fit into the rules or format, but we do the best we can. Type of material in the fixed field is coded here as "i" for pictures.

Example 53: Environmental Values Action Cards

```
Type:        k Bib lvl: m Source:     d Lang:   eng
Type mat:  o Enc lvl: I Govt pub:      Ctry:   mnu
Int lvl:   c Mod rec:   Tech:       n Leng:   nnn
Desc:        a Accomp:     Dat tp:    s Dates: 1976,
 1 040        XXX ǂc XXX
 2 007        k ǂb o ǂd b ǂe c
 3 090        BF408
 4 092 0      153.42 ǂ2 20
 5 049        XXXX
 6 245 00     Environmental values action cards ǂh flash card
 7 260        [Saint Paul, Minn.] : ǂb Minnesota Dept. of Education,
ǂc 1976.
 8 300        50 activity cards : ǂb b&w ; ǂc 21 x 21 cm.
 9 500        Project director: Richard C. Clark.
10 500        On the back of each photograph or illustration are
suggested activities.
11 520        Intended to help children explore their values, become
aware of themselves, and express their ideas creatively.
*12 650   0   Creative thinking.
13 650   0   Social values.
14 650   0   Self-perception.
15 650   8   Creative thinking.
16 650   8   Self perception.
17 650   8   Social values.
18 700  11   Clark, Richard C.
19 710  11   Minnesota. ǂb Dept. of Education.
```

I used value "o" (flash card) for type of material, because I consider activity cards to be a type of flash card.

Example 54: Mexico, Crafts and Industries

```
Type:       k Bib lvl: m Source:    d Lang:   eng
Type mat: i Enc lvl: I Govt pub:    Ctry:    ilu
Int lvl:  c Mod rec:   Tech:      n Leng:   nnn
Desc:       a Accomp:    Dat tp:    s Dates: 1968,
 1 040      XXX ǂc XXX
 2 007      k ǂb f ǂd c ǂe c
 3 043      n-mx---
 4 090      F1210
 5 092 0    338.0972 ǂ2 19
 6 049      XXXX
 7 245 00   Mexico, crafts and industries ǂh picture / ǂc produced
by Society for Visual Education.
 8 260      Chicago, Ill. : ǂb SVE, ǂc c1968.
 9 300      8 study prints : ǂb col. ; ǂc 23 x 46 cm. in
portfolio.
10 440 0    Mexico, Central America, and the West Indies today
11 500      Consultant: Carroll J. Schwartz.
13 500      Notes, research questions, enrichment activities, key
words, maps, picture, and list of related filmstrips on back of
study prints.
14 505 0    Pottery painters at work -- Silversmith at work --
Building with adobe bricks -- Drying sisal -- Printing textiles --
Fishermen at work -- Refining petroleum -- Port of Veracruz.
15 651  0   Mexico ǂx Industries.
16 651  8   Mexico ǂx Industries.
17 700 11   Schwartz, Carroll J.
18 710 21   Society for Visual Education.
```

Fixed field "Int lvl" is coded "c" for elementary and junior high.
In field 007, subfield ǂe is coded "c" for cardboard.

Example 55: Transportation

```
Type:      k Bib lvl: m Source:    d Lang:   eng
Type mat: i Enc lvl: I Govt pub:    Ctry:   wiu
Int lvl:  e Mod rec:   Tech:     n Leng:   nnn
Desc:      a Accomp:    Dat tp:   q Dates: 1970,1979
 1 040      XXX ǂc XXX
 2 007      k ǂb i ǂd b ǂe c
 3 043      n-us-wi
 4 045      w7x3
 5 090      HE151
 6 092 0    380.50973 ǂ2 19
 7 049      XXXX
 8 245 00   Transportation ǂh picture / ǂc the State Historical
Society of Wisconsin.
 9 260      [Madison, Wis.] : ǂb The Society, ǂc [197-?]
10 300      23 reproductions of photographs : ǂb b&w ; ǂc 22 x 28
cm. + ǂe 1 guidesheet.
11 500      Title on guidesheet: Transportation in the 1890's.
12 520      Photographs from 1870 to 1930 of streetcars, excursion
boats and schooners, bicycles, stagecoaches, trolleys, early
automobiles and buses, railroad parlor cars, horse-drawn buggies,
sleds, sleighs, carts, fire and hose wagons, milk wagons, school
buses, and streetcars.
13 650  0   Transportation ǂz United States ǂx History.
14 650  8   Transportation ǂx History.
15 710 21   State Historical Society of Wisconsin.
16 740 01   Transportation in the 1890's.
```

Example 56: Portrait of Mister Rogers

```
Type:       k Bib lvl: m Source:     d Lang:   eng
Type mat: i Enc lvl: I Govt pub:     Ctry:  xxu
Int lvl:  f Mod rec:    Tech:      n Leng:   nnn
Desc:       a Accomp:     Dat tp:   s Dates: 1984,
 1 040       xxx ǂc xxx
 2 007       k ǂb i ǂd c ǂe o
 3 090       PN1992.3.R6
 4 092 0     921 ǂ2 19
 5 049       xxxx
 6 245 00    [Portrait of Mister Rogers] ǂh picture
 7 260       $c [1984?]
 8 300       1 photograph : ǂb col. ; ǂc 13 x 18 cm.
 9 500       Photograph of Fred Rogers of the television program
Mister Rogers' neighborhood.
10 500       Title supplied by cataloger.
11 500       Inscription: For Nancy with kindest regards and
gratitude for your help with our "history." Fred Rogers, 1984,
"Mister Rogers."
12 600 10    Rogers, Fred.
13 600 18    Rogers, Fred.
14 700 11    Rogers, Fred.
```

This unpublished item has only subfield ǂc in field 260.

Example 57: Motivational Curriculum Chart

```
Type:       k Bib lvl: m Source:     d Lang:   eng
Type mat: n Enc lvl: I Govt pub:     Ctry:  cau
Int lvl:  f Mod rec:    Tech:      n Leng:   nnn
Desc:       a Accomp:     Dat tp:   s Dates: 1969,
 1 040       xxx ǂc xxx
 2 007       k ǂb n ǂd b ǂe o
 3 090       LB1570
 4 092 0     375.001 ǂ2 20
 5 049       xxxx
 6 100 1     Cherry, Clare.
 7 245 10    Motivational curriculum chart. ǂn No. 1, ǂp For early
childhood ǂh chart / ǂc by Clare Cherry.
 8 260       Belmont, CA : ǂb Fearon, ǂc c1969.
 9 300       1 chart : ǂb b&w ; ǂc 48 x 61 cm. folded to 18 x 31
cm.
10 520       Chart has 54 horizontal rows divided into 7 general
areas of learning. The 17 columns contain specific activity
suggestions. Designed to be used as a motivational reminder for
curriculum planning.
11 650  0    Curriculum planning.
12 650  8    Education ǂx Curricula.
13 710 21    Fearon Publishers.
```

Notice the coding of field 245. This pattern of subfields ǂa, ǂn, ǂp often is encountered in sets of videorecordings.
In field 007, subfield ǂb is coded "n" for chart.

Example 58: Public access to government documents

```
Type:       k Bib lvl: m Source:     d Lang:    eng
Type mat: i Enc lvl: I Govt pub:     Ctry:    dcu
Int lvl:  g Mod rec:   Tech:       n Leng:    nnn
Desc:       a Accomp:     Dat tp:    s Dates: 1975,
   1 040     XXX ǂc XXX
   2 007     k ǂb f ǂd c ǂe o
   3 043     n-us---
   4 090     KF4774
   5 092 0   323.445 ǂ2 19
   6 049     XXXX
   7 100 1   Buchanan, William W.
   8 245 10  "Public access to government documents is essential to
the successful operation of a democracy".
   9 260     Washington, D.C. : ǂb United States Historical
Documents Institute, ǂc c1975.
  10 300     1 poster : ǂb col. ; ǂc 76 x 56 cm.
  11 500     Poster designed as sales promotion for sets of indexes
to government documents; used during the U.S. Bicentennial year.
  12 500     Quotation by William S. Moorhead, Congressman from
Pennsylvania. Poster copyright by William W. Buchanan.
  13 500     Red, white, and blue books arranged like stripes and
star field of American flag, on dark blue background.
  14 650 0   Freedom of information.
  15 650 0   Government publications.
  16 650 8   Freedom of information.
  17 650 8   Government publications.
* 18 700 11  Moorhead, William S. ǂq (William Singer), ǂd 1923-
  19 710 21  United States Historical Documents Institute.
```

"Type mat" value "i" for pictures is used as the closest value for this poster. In field 007, subfield ǂb is coded "f" because that value includes posters.

Example 59: The Black Cat

```
Type:        k Bib lvl: m Source:    d Lang:    eng
Type mat: i Enc lvl: I Govt pub:    Ctry:    cau
Int lvl:   g Mod rec:    Tech:     n Leng:    nnn
Desc:        a Accomp:    Dat tp:    s Dates: 1976,
  1 040        XXX ǂc XXX
  2 007        k ǂb f ǂd c ǂe o
  3 090        PN1995.9.H6
  4 092 0      813.3 ǂ2 20
  5 049        XXXX
  6 245 00  Carl Laemmle presents Karloff and Bela Lugosi in Edgar
Allan Poe's The black cat ǂh picture
  7 260        Corte Madera, Calif. : ǂb Portal Publications, ǂc
c1976.
  8 300        1 poster : ǂb col. ; ǂc 74 x 48 cm.
  9 500        Reproduction of poster for 1934 movie by Universal
Pictures.
 10 650   0  Horror films.
 11 650   0  Film posters.
 12 650   8  Horror ǂx Motion pictures.
 13 600 10  Poe, Edgar Allan, ǂd 1809-1849. ǂt Black cat.
 14 700 11  Laemmle, Carl, ǂd 1867-1939.
 15 700 11  Karloff, Boris, ǂd 1887-1969.
 16 700 11  Lugosi, Bela, ǂd 1882-1956.
 17 710 21  Universal Pictures Company.
*18 710 21  Portal Publications Ltd.
 19 730 01  Black cat (Motion picture)
```

There is no subfield code before the qualifier in line 19. In field 007, subfield ǂe is coded "o" for paper.

Example 60: Division

```
Type:        k Bib lvl: m Source:    d Lang:    eng
Type mat: o Enc lvl: I Govt pub:    Ctry:    ilu
Int lvl:   b Mod rec:    Tech:     n Leng:    nnn
Desc:        a Accomp:    Dat tp:    s Dates: 1963,
  1 040        XXX ǂc XXX
  2 007        k ǂb o ǂd b ǂe c
  3 090        QA115
  4 092 0      513.214 ǂ2 20
  5 049        XXXX
  6 245 00  Division ǂh flash card
  7 260        Chicago, Ill. : ǂb Ideal School Supply Co., ǂc 1963.
  8 300        90 flash cards : ǂb b&w ; ǂc 8 x 23 cm.
  9 440   0  New math flash cards
 10 500        Title from container.
 11 500        "No. 789."
 12 650   0  Division.
 13 650   0  Arithmetic.
 14 650   8  Division.
 15 710 21  Ideal School Supply Company.
```

Value "o" for fixed field "Type mat" is for flash cards.

Example 61: The Human Skull

```
Type:       k Bib lvl: m Source:     d Lang:  eng
Type mat: i Enc lvl: I Govt pub:    Ctry:   enk
Int lvl:  f Mod rec:   Tech:      n Leng:  nnn
Desc:       a Accomp:     Dat tp:   s Dates: 1980,
 1  040      XXX ‡c XXX
 2  007      k ‡b f ‡d a ‡e o
 3  090      QM105
 4  092 0    611.91 ‡2 20
 5  049      XXXX
 6  100 1    Miller, Richard.
 7  245 14   The human skull.
 8  260      London : ‡b Fisher-Miller, ‡c 1980.
 9  300      1 drawing : ‡b brown & tan ; ‡c 46 x 64 cm. + ‡e 1
sheet of assembly instructions.
10  500      Design and copyright by Richard Miller; to be
assembled into model of human skull.
11  650 0    Skull.
12  650 0    Head.
13  650 8    Anatomy, Human.
14  650 8    Head.
15  710 21   Fisher-Miller (Firm)
```

The value "i" (picture) in fixed field "Type mat" is not quite right, but it seemed the closest of the few possibilities.

Example 62: Common Loon

```
Type:       k Bib lvl: m Source:     d Lang:  eng
Type mat: c Enc lvl: I Govt pub:    Ctry:   mnu
Int lvl:  f Mod rec:   Tech:      n Leng:  nnn
Desc:       a Accomp:     Dat tp:   q Dates: 1980,1983
 1  040      XXX ‡c XXX
 2  007      k ‡b f ‡d c ‡e o
 3  090      QL696
 4  092 0    598.442 ‡2 20
 5  049      XXXX
 6  100 1    Loates, Martin Glen, ‡d 1945-
 7  245 10   Common loon ‡h art reproduction / ‡c M.G. Loates.
 8  260      Kenyon, Minn. : ‡b Nature Incentives, U.S.A., ‡c [198-
?]
 9  300      1 art reproduction : ‡b col. ; ‡c 36 x 31 cm. in mat
51 x 41 cm.
10  500      Watercolor of loon head with sketches of loon.
12  500      Sketch in lower right labeled: Tail and wing movement
diving.
13  650 0    Loons.
14  650 8    Loons.
15  710 21   Nature Incentives, U.S.A.
```

"Type mat" is coded "c" for art reproductions. In field 007, subfield ‡b, value "f" includes art reproductions.

Example 63: Common Loons

```
Type:       k Bib lvl: m Source:    d Lang:   eng
Type mat: a Enc lvl: I Govt pub:    Ctry:   iau
Int lvl:  f Mod rec:   Tech:    n Leng:   nnn
Desc:     a Accomp:    Dat tp:   s Dates: 1982,
 1 040      XXX ‡c XXX
 2 007      k ‡b e ‡d c ‡e o
 3 090      QL696.G33
 4 092 0    598.442 ‡2 20
 5 049      XXXX
 6 100 1    Danbom, Carroll D.
 7 245 10   Common loons ‡h art original / ‡c C. Danbom.
 8 260      ‡c 1982.
 9 300      1 art original : ‡b pastel on paper ; ‡c visible image
32 x 43 cm. in frame 50 x 60 cm.
10 500      Signed on back: Common loons, a pastel by Carroll D.
Danbom.
11 650   0  Loons.
12 650   8  Loons.
```

"Type mat" is coded "a" for art originals. In field 007, subfield ‡b, value "e" is for a painting.

COMPUTER FILES

AACR 2 Chapter 9

Example 64: MacInTax 1989

```
Type:      m Bib lvl: m Source:   d Lang:    eng
File:      b Enc lvl: I Govt pub:   Ctry:    cau
Audience: f Mod rec:   Frequn:   n Regulr:
Desc:      a            Dat tp:   s Dates:  1989,
 1 010
 2 040      XXX ǂc XXX
 3 090      HJ4652
 4 092 0    336.24 ǂ2 20
 5 049      XXXX
 6 245 00   MacInTax 1989 ǂh computer file
 7 250      Version v1.1.1.
 8 260      Oxnard, Calif. : ǂb SoftView, ǂc c1989.
 9 300      4 computer disks ; ǂc 3 1/2 in. + ǂe 1 user's guide.
10 538      System requirements: Macintosh 512KE; printer.
11 500      Title from title screen.
12 520      Designed to aid user in preparing federal income tax return.
Performs calculations, moves results to appropriate forms, and prints
completed forms.
13 650  0   Income tax ǂz United States.
14 710 20   SoftView, Inc.
15 753      Macintosh 512KE.
```

At the Annual Conference of the American Library Asociation in June 1992, the MARBI committee considered Discussion paper no. 56, "Coding Languages for Computer Files." It was agreed that the language of the *screen displays* should be coded in the fixed fields. These examples all have been changed from the previous coding of "N/A" in the fixed field "Lang."

For all examples —

* Changed from form appearing in *Cataloging of Audiovisual Materials*, 3d edition. LC authority file searched June 1992.

** Cataloging changed.

Example 65A: Aldus PageMaker

```
Type:      m Bib lvl: m Source:    d Lang:    eng
File:      b Enc lvl: I Govt pub:    Ctry:    wau
Audience: f Mod rec:    Frequn:    n Regulr:
Desc:      a            Dat tp:    s Dates:   1990,
 1 010
 2 040       XXX ‡c XXX
 3 090       Z286.D47
 4 092 0     005.3 ‡2 20
 5 049       XXXX
 6 245 00    Aldus PageMaker 4.0 ‡h computer file
 7 250       Version 4.0.
 8 260       Seattle, WA : ‡b Aldus, ‡c c1990.
 9 300       4 computer disks : ‡b col. ; ‡c 3 1/2 in. + ‡e 5 manuals + 1
training package.
10 538       Systems requirements: Macintosh Plus, SE family, or Mac II
family; 1-2MB RAM; system version 6.05; hard disk with minimum of 5MB;
laser printer.
11 500       Title from title screen; title on box: Aldus PageMaker.
12 500       Includes reference manual, "getting started" manual,
including quick reference guide, introduction to PageMaker, table editor
guide, and templates guide.
13 500       Training package includes 1 computer disk, 1 sound cassette,
1 command summary card.
14 520       A desktop publishing package allowing the user to integrate
text and graphics and to control the appearance of documents.
15 650  0    Desktop publishing.
16 650  0    Printing, Practical.
17 710 20    Aldus Corporation.
18 730 01    Aldus PageMaker.
19 740 01    PageMaker.
20 740 01    Page maker.
21 753       Macintosh Plus.
22 753       Macintosh SE.
23 753       Macintosh II.
```

Field 538 has only subfield ‡a.

Example 65B: PageMaker 4 by Example

```
Type: a        Bib lvl: m Source:    d Lang:   eng
Repr:          Enc lvl: I Conf pub: o Ctry:    cau
Indx: o        Mod rec:   Govt pub:   Cont:
Desc: a        Int lvl:   Festschr: o Illus: a
               F/B:     o Dat tp:    s Dates: 1990,
    1 010
    2 040      XXX ‡c XXX
    3 090      Z286.D47
    4 092 0    005.3 ‡2 20
    5 049      XXXX
**  6 100 1    Webster, David, ‡d 1967-
**  7 245 00   PageMaker 4 by example, Macintosh version / ‡c David
Webster, Tony Webster ; adapted to PageMaker 4 by Paul Webster and
Carolyn Webster.
    8 250      1st ed.
    9 260      Redwood City, Calif. : ‡b M&T Books, ‡c c1990.
   10 300      593 p. : ‡b ill. ; ‡c 24 cm. + ‡e 1 computer disk (3 1/2
in.)
   11 500      Systems requirements: Macintosh Plus, SE, II; hard disk;
PageMaker computer program version 4.0.
   12 500      Cover title: PageMaker 4 by example for the Macintosh.
   13 500      Includes index.
   14 500      Computer disk contains self-paced exercises.
   15 630 00   PageMaker (Computer program)
   16 650  0   Desktop publishing.
** 17 700 10   Webster, Tony, ‡d 1940-
** 18 700 10   Webster, Paul.
   19 700 10   Webster, Carolyn.
   20 740 01   PageMaker four by example, Macintosh version.
   21 740 01   PageMaker 4 by example for the Macintosh.
```

Field 538 is not valid in the books format, so we use field 500 for the systems requirement note. Field 538 will be available for this use after format integration.

Example 66: Image Gallery

```
Type:       m Bib lvl: m Source:    d Lang:     eng
File:       b Enc lvl: I Govt pub:    Ctry:     xxu
Audience: f Mod rec:     Frequn:    n Regulr:
Desc:       a             Dat tp:    s Dates:    1990,
 1 010
 2 040      XXX ǂc XXX
 3 090      Z286.D47
 4 092 0    005.3 ǂ2 20
 5 049      XXXX
 6 245 00   Image gallery ǂh computer file / ǂc NEC.
 7 250      Version 1.1.
 8 260      [United States] : ǂb NEC, ǂc c1989.
 9 300      1 computer disk ; ǂc 4 3/4 in. + ǂe 1 user's manual.
10 538      Systems requirements: Macintosh 512E, Plus, SE, or II;
desktop publishing software; CD-ROM reader.
11 500      Images by Metro ImageBase, Inc.
12 500      User's manual shows each image.
13 520      Includes "2,800 professionally hand-drawn images" divided
among 20 categories; in TIFF or EPS file format, for use in desktop
publishing.
14 650  0   Desktop publishing.
15 650  0   Copy art.
* 16 710 20  NEC Electronics.
17 710 20   Metro ImageBase, Inc.
18 740 01   NEC Image gallery.
19 753      Macintosh 512E.
```

"Audience" in the fixed field is coded "f" for "specialized" for this type of computer file.

Example 67: Ludwig van Beethoven Symphony no. 9

```
Type:      m Bib lvl: m Source:   d Lang:    eng
File:      b Enc lvl: I Govt pub:   Ctry:    cau
Audience: f Mod rec:   Frequn:   n Regulr:
Desc:      a            Dat tp:   s Dates:   1991,
```

```
 1 010
 2 040        XXX ǂc XXX
 3 090        M1001.B4 Op.125
 4 049        XXXX
 5 245 00     Ludwig van Beethoven Symphony no. 9 ǂh computer file
 6 250        Upgraded version.
 7 260        Santa Monica, Calif. : ǂb Voyager, ǂc c1991.
 8 300        1 computer disk : ǂb sd. ; ǂc 4 3/4 in. + ǂe 1 user's guide.
 9 440  0     CD companion series
10 500        Interactive media.
11 538        Systems requirements: Macintosh Plus, SE, or II; HyperCard
2.0; hard disk drive; CD-ROM drive, earphones or speakers.
12 500        Title from container.
13 500        Program by Robert Winter ; program design by Robert Winter,
Robert Stein.
14 500        Music recorded: Symphony no. 9 / Ludwig van Beethoven.
London: Decca, c1988. Joan Sutherland, soprano ; Marilyn Horne,
contralto ; James King, tenor ; Martti Talvela, bass ; Vienna State
Opera Chorus, Wilhelm Pitz, chorus master ; Vienna Philharmonic, Hans
Schmidt-Issersdtedt, conductor. Originally released by Decca, 1966.
15 520        Allows user to examine the music itself along with the
historical and personal setting in which it was created. Features
include detailed real-time commentary on the entire work and explanation
of music showing excerpts from the score.
16 600 10     Beethoven, Ludwig van, ǂd 1770-1827. ǂt Symphonies, ǂn no.
9, op. 125, ǂr D minor ǂx Analysis, appreciation.
17 650  0     Music appreciation.
18 650  0     Musical analysis.
19 650  0     Music ǂy 19th century ǂx History and criticism.
20 700 10     Winter, Robert, ǂd 1945-
21 700 10     Stein, Robert.
22 700 10     Beethoven, Ludwig van, ǂd 1770-1827. ǂt Symphonies, ǂn no.
9, op. 125, ǂr D minor. ǂf 1988.
```

Fields 600 and 700 are coded as in the score or sound recording format.

Example 68: Quarterstaff

```
Type:      m Bib lvl: m Source:     d Lang:     eng
File:      b Enc lvl: I Govt pub:    Ctry:     mau
Audience: f Mod rec:   Frequn:     n Regulr:
Desc:      a            Dat tp:     s Dates:    1988,
 1 010
 2 040       XXX ‡c XXX
 4 090       GV1469.25.Q3
 5 092 0     793.932 ‡2 20
 6 049       XXXX
 7 245 00    Quarterstaff ‡h computer file : ‡b the tomb of Setmoth / ‡c
written by Scott Schmitz & Ken Updike ; produced by Christopher Erhardt.
 8 260       Cambridge, MA : ‡b Infocom, ‡c c1988.
 9 300       3 computer disks : ‡b sd., col. ; ‡c 3 1/2 in. + ‡e 1 user's
manual + 1 reference guide + 1 chart + 1 wooden token + 1 poster.
10 500       Role-playing game.
11 538       System requirements: Mac Plus, SE or II; 2MB memory; color
video card.
12 500       Title from title screen.
13 520       "Three months ago, the Tree Druid colony vanished without a
trace. It is your mission--and that of your companions--to discover what
fate has befallen these gentle souls, and to save any that may survive"-
-Container.
14 650  0    Fantasy games.
15 650  0    Computer adventure games.
16 700 10    Schmitz, Scott.
17 700 10    Updike, Ken.
18 700 10    Erhardt, Christopher.
* 19 710 20  Infocom (Firm)
```

Here we have field 300 subfield ‡e with lots of things listed in it—but all in one subfield.

Example 69:   The Manhole

```
Type:       m Bib lvl: m Source:    d Lang:     eng
File:       b Enc lvl: I Govt pub:   Ctry:     mau
Audience: f Mod rec:    Frequn:   n Regulr:
Desc:       a            Dat tp:   c Dates:   1989,1988
 1 010
 2 040       XXX ǂc XXX
 3 090       GV1469.2
 4 092 0     793.932 ǂ2 20
 5 049       XXXX
 6 245 04    The Manhole ǂh computer file / ǂc Cyan ; [developed by Robyn
Miller and Rand Miller] ; produced by Christopher Erhardt.
 7 260       Menlo Park, CA : ǂb Activision ; ǂb distributed by
Mediagenic, ǂc 1989, c1988.
 8 300       1 computer disk ; ǂb sd., col. ; ǂc 4 3/4 in.
 9 500       "A fantasy exploration for children of all ages."
10 538       System requirements: Macintosh Plus, SE, or II; 1 megabyte
of memory; HyperCard 1.2.1 or higher; SCSI hard drive, Apple CD-SC CD-
ROM drive or equivalent.
11 500       Title from title screens.
12 650  0    Computer games.
13 650  0    Fantasy games.
14 700 10    Miller, Robyn.
15 700 10    Miller, Rand.
16 700 10    Whiteley, Sherry.
17 710 20    Cyan Software.
18 710 20    Activision, Inc.
19 710 20    Mediagenic (Firm)
20 753       Macintosh Plus.
```

Subfield ǂb is repeated in field 260 for the distribution statement.

Example 70: Stoneware's DB Master

```
Type:       m Bib lvl: m Source:    d Lang:    eng
File:       b Enc lvl: I Govt pub:   Ctry:    cau
Audience: f Mod rec:    Frequn:    n Regulr:
Desc:       a            Dat tp:    s Dates:  1982,
 1 040       XXX ǂc XXX
 2 090       QA76.9.D3
 3 092 0     005.74 ǂ2 20
 4 049       XXXX
 5 245 00    Stoneware's DB master ǂh computer file
 6 250       Version three, Apple II ed., rev. 3.02.
 7 260       San Rafael, CA : ǂb Stoneware, ǂc 1982.
 8 300       2 computer disks ; ǂc 5 1/4 in. + ǂe 1 manual.
 9 500       Data base management program.
10 538       System requirements: Apple II or higher; two disk
drives, printer.
11 500       Title from title screen; title on manual: D B master.
12 500       Second disk is back-up.
13 650   0   Data base management.
14 650   8   Information systems ǂx Computer programs.
15 710 20    Stoneware, Inc.
16 740 01    DB master.
17 740 01    D B master.
18 753       Apple II.
```

All the version/edition information goes into one field 250.

Example 71A: Alphabet Zoo

```
Type:       m Bib lvl: m Source:    d Lang:     eng
File:       b Enc lvl: I Govt pub:     Ctry:    mau
Audience: b Mod rec:     Frequn:    n Regulr:
Desc:       a              Dat tp:    s Dates:   1983,
 1 040       XXX ‡c XXX
 2 090       PE1143
 3 092 0     421.52 ‡2 20
 4 049       XXXX
 5 100 1     Disharoon, Dale.
 6 245 10    Alphabet zoo ‡h computer file / ‡c by Dale Disharoon ;
artwork by Bill Groetzinger.
 7 260       Cambridge, Mass. : ‡b Spinnaker Software Corp., ‡c
c1983.
 8 300       1 computer disk : ‡b sd., col. ; ‡c 5 1/4 in. + ‡e 1
user's guide.
 9 440  0    Early learning series
10 538       System requirements: Apple II.
11 500       Title from title screens.
12 500       James Bach, Scott Bailey, programmers.
13 500       For children 3 to 8 years old.
14 505 0     ABC time -- Letter game -- Spelling zoo.
15 650  0    English language ‡x Orthography and spelling.
16 650  8    English language ‡x Spelling.
17 700 10    Bailey, Scott.
18 700 10    Bach, James.
19 710 20    Spinnaker Software Corp.
20 740 01    ABC time.
21 740 01    Letter game.
22 740 01    Spelling zoo.
23 753       Apple II.
```

The "Audience" value is coded "b" for kindergarten through 3rd grade.

Example 71B: ABC time

```
Type:       m Bib lvl: m Source:   d Lang:    eng
File:       b Enc lvl: I Govt pub:   Ctry:    mau
Audience: b Mod rec:    Frequn:   n Regulr:
Desc:       a             Dat tp:   s Dates:  1983,
 1 040      XXX ‡c XXX
 2 090      PE1143
 3 092 0    421.52 ‡2 20
 4 049      XXXX
 5 100 1    Disharoon, Dale.
 6 245 10   ABC time ‡h computer file
 7 300      on 1 computer disk : ‡b sd., col. ; ‡c 5 1/4 in. + ‡e
1 user's guide.
 8 538      System requirements: Apple II.
 9 500      Title from title screens.
10 500      For children 3 to 8 years old.
11 520      Shows each letter of the alphabet and draws a picture
to go with it. Player presses letter on keyboard to match letter
on the screen.
12 650  0   English language ‡x Orthography and spelling.
13 700 10   Bach, James.
14 700 10   Bailey, Scott.
15 710 20   Spinnaker Software Corp.
16 753      Apple II.
17 773 0    ‡7 p1mm ‡a Disharoon, Dale. ‡t Alphabet zoo. ‡d
Cambridge, Mass. : Spinnaker Software, c1983. ‡w (OCoLC)nnnnnnn
```

Field 773 would generate an "In" analytic note on a catalog card.

Example 72: President Elect

```
Type:      m Bib lvl: m Source:    d Lang:     eng
File:      b Enc lvl: I Govt pub:    Ctry:     cau
Audience: d Mod rec:    Frequn:    n Regulr:
Desc:      a            Dat tp:    s Dates:    1981,
 1 040     XXX ǂc XXX
 2 043     n-us---
 3 090     JK524
 4 092 0   324.973 ǂ2 20
 5 049     XXXX
 6 100 1   Hernandez, Nelson G.
 7 245 10  President elect ǂh computer file / ǂc by Nelson G.
Hernandez.
 8 260     Mountain View, CA : ǂb Strategic Simulations, ǂc
c1981.
 9 300     1 computer disk : ǂb sd., col. ; ǂc 5 1/4 in. + ǂe 1
rule book + 1 short rule card + 1 pad of campaign strategy sheets.
10 538     System requirements: Apple II or higher.
11 500     Title from title screen.
12 520     Simulation for one to three players of presidential
campaigning from Labor Day to election night; players decide how
to allocate campaign funds. Includes six historical scenarios,
hypothetical scenarios, and minute-by-minute election returns.
13 650  0  Presidents ǂz United States ǂx Election.
14 650  8  Elections ǂz United States.
15 710 20  Strategic Simulations, Inc.
16 753     Apple II.
```

Field 043 is coded for the geographic coverage.

Example 73: Lode Runner

```
Type:      m Bib lvl: m Source:    d Lang:     eng
File:      b Enc lvl: I Govt pub:   Ctry:     cau
Audience: d Mod rec:   Frequn:    n Regulr:
Desc:      a             Dat tp:   s Dates:   1983,
 1 040      XXX ǂc XXX
 2 090      GV1469.35.L6
 3 092 0    749.8 ǂ2 20
 4 049      XXXX
 5 100 1    Smith, Doug.
 6 240 10   Lode runner
 7 245 00   Broderbund Software presents Lode runner ǂh computer
file / ǂc by Doug Smith.
 8 260      San Rafael, Calif. : ǂb Broderbund Software, ǂc c1983.
 9 300      1 computer disk : ǂb sd., col. ; ǂc 5 1/4 in. + ǂe 1
set of directions.
10 500      System requirements: Apple II or higher.
11 538      Title from title screen; title in directions:
Loderunner.
12 520      Action game and game generator for one player. Game
has 150 different puzzles or mazes. Game generator permits player
to design puzzles and scenes.
13 650  0   Video games.
14 650  8   Video games.
15 710 20   Broderbund Software.
16 740 01   Loderunner.
17 753      Apple II.
```

The uniform title is entered in field 240.

Example 74: Speedway

```
Type:       m Bib lvl: m Source:    d Lang:     eng
File:       b Enc lvl: I Govt pub:    Ctry:     cau
Audience: c Mod rec:    Frequn:    n Regulr:
Desc:       a             Dat tp:    s Dates:    1978,
 1 040      XXX ǂc XXX
 2 090      GV1469.35.S6
 3 092 0    794.8 ǂ2 20
 4 049      XXXX
 5 245 00   Speedway!. Spin-out!. Crypto-logic! ǂh computer file
 6 253      Programs.
 7 260      [Los Angeles] : ǂb North American Philips Consumer
Electronics, ǂc c1978.
 8 300      1 computer chip cartridge : ǂb sd., col. ; ǂc 3 1/4
in. + ǂe 1 set of official rules.
 9 538      System requirements: Odyssey2 game system.
10 500      Title from cartridge label.
11 520      Three games for one or more players. The first two are
car racing games, the third (for two players) involves solving
secret messages.
12 650  0   Racing.
13 650  0   Video games.
14 650  0   Cryptography.
15 650  8   Video games.
16 710 20   North American Philips Consumer Electronics Corp.
17 730 01   Speedway! ǂf 1978.
18 730 01   Spin-out! ǂf 1978.
19 730 01   Crypto-logic! ǂf 1978.
20 753      Odyssey2 game system.
```

All the titles are in subfield ǂa of field 245. Individual uniform title added entries (730) are used to provide access to the individual titles.

THREE-DIMENSIONAL ARTEFACTS AND REALIA

AACR 2 Chapter 10

Example 75: Minnesota Trivia

```
Type:      r Bib lvl: m Source:     d Lang:   eng
Type mat: g Enc lvl: I Govt pub:    Ctry:    mnu
Int lvl:  g Mod rec:   Tech:      n Leng:    nnn
Desc:      a Accomp:     Dat tp:   s Dates:  1984,
 1 010
 2 040      XXX ǂc XXX
 3 090      F606.5
 4 092 0    917 ǂa 793.73
 5 049      XXXX
 6 245 00   Minnesota trivia ǂh game
 7 260      Minnetonka, MN : ǂb Minnesota Trivia, ǂc c1984.
 8 300      1 game ; ǂc in box 27 x 27 x 9 cm.
 9 500      Includes 1 game board, 4 markers, 1 die, 500 question/answer
cards, 2 card boxes, 28 scoring cards, 1 rule sheet.
10 520      Game for two or more players or teams in which players must
answer Minnesota-related questions on people, places, sports, or "pot-
luck" to move from city to city on the board.
11 650  0   Board games.
12 651  0   Minnesota ǂx History.
13 650  0   Educational games.
14 710 20   Minnesota Trivia, Inc.
```

For all examples —

* Changed from form appearing in *Cataloging of Audiovisual Materials,* 3d edition. LC authority file searched June 1992.

** Cataloging changed.

Example 76: Cathedral

```
Type:       r Bib lvl: m Source:     d Lang:    eng
Type mat: g Enc lvl: I Govt pub:     Ctry:    nz
Int lvl:  g Mod rec:   Tech:      n Leng:    nnn
Desc:       a Accomp:     Dat tp:   s Dates: 1985,
 1 010
 2 040       XXX ǂc XXX
 3 090       GV1469.C3
 4 092 0     793.9 ǂ2 20
 5 049       XXXX
 6 245 00    Cathedral ǂh game : ǂb the game of the mediaeval city.
 7 250  0    3rd ed.
 8 260       [New Zealand? : ǂb s.n.], ǂc 1985.
 9 300       1 game (playing board, 30 pieces, rules book) : ǂb wood ; ǂc
in box 26 x 26 x 7 cm.
10 500       Game for two players or teams.
11 500       Copyright by Robert P. Moore.
12 520       Based upon the concept of a medieval city surrounded by a
wall with a cathedral as focal point, place of sanctuary, and mediator
in keeping any one faction from becoming too powerful. Playing pieces
are buildings; opponents attempt to gain control of property within the
city.
13 650  0    Games.
14 650  0    Board games.
15 700 10    Moore, Robert P.
```

There is field 007 for materials cataloged according to chapter 10.

Example 77: Monopoly

```
Type:       r Bib lvl: m Source:    d Lang:   eng
Type mat: g Enc lvl: I Govt pub:    Ctry:    mau
Int lvl:  g Mod rec:   Tech:      n Leng:   nnn
Desc:       a Accomp:     Dat tp:  s Dates: 1985,
 1 010
 2 040       XXX ǂc XXX
 3 090       GV1469.M65
 4 092 0     793.7 ǂ2 20
 5 049       XXXX
 6 245 00    Monopoly ǂh game
 7 250       Deluxe anniversary ed.
 8 260       Beverly, MA : ǂb Parker Brothers, ǂc c1985.
 9 300       1 game (various pieces) ; ǂc in container 26 x 51 x 7 cm.
10 500       "Parker Brothers real estate trading game" for 2 to 8
players.
11 500       Includes game board, play money, 2 dice, 11 gold-colored
playing pieces, red wooden hotels, green wooden houses, title deed
cards, chance and community chest cards, rules.
12 500       Rule book includes illustrated 50-year history of the game.
13 520       "The object of the game is to become the wealthiest player
through buying, renting, and selling property."
14 650  0    Monopoly (Game).
15 650  0    Board games.
16 710 21    Parker Brothers, Inc.
```

The qualifier in field 650 does not have a subfield code before it.

Example 78: Human Skull

```
Type:       r Bib lvl: m Source:    d Lang:   eng
Type mat: q Enc lvl: I Govt pub:    Ctry:    xxu
Int lvl:  f Mod rec:   Tech:      n Leng:   nnn
Desc:       a Accomp:     Dat tp:  s Dates: 1983,
 1 040       XXX ǂc XXX
 2 090       QM105
 3 092 0     611.91 ǂ2 20
 4 049       XXXX
 5 245 00    [Human skull] ǂh model
 6 260       ǂc [1983]
 7 300       1 model : ǂb paper, tan ; ǂc 22 cm. long.
 8 500       Title supplied by cataloger.
 9 500       Assembled from: The human skull. London : Fisher-
Miller, 1980.
10 650  0    Skull.
11 650  0    Head.
12 650  8    Anatomy, Human.
13 650  8    Head.
```

No subfield codes are used in the field 500 note in line 9.

Example 79: Replicas of a Cylinder Seal Impression

```
Type:       r Bib lvl: m Source:    d Lang:    eng
Type mat: q Enc lvl: I Govt pub:    Ctry:    enk
Int lvl:   f Mod rec:   Tech:    n Leng:    nnn
Desc:       a Accomp:    Dat tp:   q Dates: 1970,1979
 1 040      XXX ‡c XXX
 2 045      b3b9
 3 090      CD5344
 4 092 0    737.6 ‡2 20
 5 049      XXXX
 6 245 00   Replica[s] of a cylinder seal impression ‡h model / ‡c
the British Museum.
 7 260      London : ‡b The Museum, ‡c [1970-?]
 8 300      5 replicas : ‡b plastic, tan on black ; ‡c 4 x 7-6 x
10 cm. on mounts 8 x 10-8 x 14 cm.
 9 500      Description on back of each replica.
10 505 0    1. An Akkadian "contest scene" (2200 B.C.) -- 2. The
seal of a scribe (Akkadian, 2200 B.C.) -- 3. An early "contest
scene" (Sumerian, 2650 B.C.) -- 4. The seal of a governor (Ur III
period, 2050 B.C.) -- 5. Seal of the scribe Adda (Akkadian, 2200
B.C.).
11 650  0   Cylinder seals.
12 650  0   Sumerians.
13 650  0   Civilization, Assyro-Babylonian.
14 650  8   Seals (Numismatics)
15 710 21   British Museum.
```

Field 045 is used for the B.C. time period represented, 2600/2699-2000/2099 B.C.

Example 80: Speedy Andrew's Repair Shop

```
Type:       r Bib lvl: m Source:    d Lang:   eng
Type mat: q Enc lvl: I Govt pub:    Ctry:   mnu
Int lvl:  f Mod rec:   Tech:      n Leng:   nnn
Desc:       a Accomp:    Dat tp:   s Dates: 1979,
  1 040       XXX ǂc XXX
  2 045       x2x3
  3 090       TL153
  4 092 0     629.286 ǂ2 20
  5 049       XXXX
  6 100 1     Olson, Andrew A., ǂd 1960-
  7 245 10    Speedy Andrew's repair shop ǂh model
  8 260       ǂe ([Lake Crystal, Minn. : ǂf A.A. Olson, ǂg 1979])
  9 300       1 model : ǂb plastic, col. ; ǂc 10 x 16 x 14 cm.
 10 500       Assembled by Andrew A. Olson from 76 piece Tyco-kit
manufactured in West Germany by Pola.
 11 520       Model of automobile repair shop of the 1920-1930
period.
* 12 650  0   Service stations.
 13 650   8   Automobiles ǂx Service stations.
```

Field 260 is coded for place, name, and date of manufacture.
The form of the first subject heading changed late in 1991.

Example 81: Geode

```
Type:       r Bib lvl: m Source: d   Lang: N/A
Type mat: r Enc lvl: I Govt pub:     Ctry: xx
Int lvl:  g Mod rec:   Tech: n       Leng: nnn
Desc:       a Accomp:    Dat tp: n   Dates:
  1 040       XXX ǂc XXX
  2 090       QE471.15.G4
  3 092 0     549 ǂ2 20
  4 049       XXXX
  5 245 00    [Geode] ǂh realia
  6 300       1 geode (2 halves) ; ǂc 4 x 5 x 4 cm.
  7 500       Title supplied by cataloger.
  8 500       Geode contains calcite crystals; from Keokuk, Iowa,
area.
  9 650  0    Geodes.
 10 650  8    Mineralogy.
 11 650  8    Rocks.
```

There is no coding for language, country, or dates for media that are not commercially packaged and distributed.

Example 82: Golden Adventure Kit of Rocks and Minerals

```
Type:       r Bib lvl: m Source:    d Lang:    eng
Type mat:   r Enc lvl: I Govt pub:    Ctry:    xxu
Int lvl:    g Mod rec:    Tech:     n Leng:    nnn
Desc:       a Accomp:      Dat tp:   s Dates:  1957,
 1 040      XXX ‡c XXX
 2 090      QE432.2
 3 092 0    549 ‡2 20
 4 049      XXXX
 5 245 00   Golden adventure kit of rocks and minerals ‡h realia
 6 260      [United States] : ‡b Golden Press, ‡c c1957.
 7 300      24 specimens ; ‡c mounted in box, 30 x 21 x 5 cm. + ‡e
1 streak plate.
 8 650   0  Rocks.
 9 650   0  Mineralogy.
10 650   8  Rocks.
11 650   8  Mineralogy.
12 710 21   Golden Press.
```

This medium is commercially distributed, so it has coding for language of the writing on the container, place of publication, and date of publication.

Example 83: Cat Skeleton

```
Type:       r Bib lvl: m Source:    d Lang:    eng
Type mat:   r Enc lvl: I Govt pub:    Ctry:    mou
Int lvl:    c Mod rec:    Tech:     n Leng:    nnn
Desc:       a Accomp:      Dat tp:   s Dates:  1968,
 1 040      XXX ‡c XXX
 2 090      QL737.C23
 3 092 0    599.74428 ‡2 20
 4 049      XXXX
 5 245 00   Cat skeleton ‡h realia : ‡b disarticulated.
**  6 260   St. Louis : ‡b Webster Division, McGraw-Hill, ‡c 1968.
 7 300      1 skeleton ; ‡c in box, 17 x 11 x 8 cm. + ‡e 1
teacher's guide (72 p. ; 28 cm).
 8 440   0  Bones
 9 440   0  Elementary science study
10 520   8  Bones of a cat; to be assembled into a skeleton.
11 500      "18512"
12 650   0  Cats ‡x Anatomy.
13 650   8  Cats ‡x Anatomy.
```

Fixed field "Int lvl" is coded "c" because the series is designed for elementary school students. It could be coded "f" for specialized, because other age groups could use this.

Example 84: Dig

```
Type:       r Bib lvl: m Source:    d Lang:    eng
Type mat: g Enc lvl: I Govt pub:    Ctry:    cau
Int lvl:  d Mod rec:   Tech:      n Leng:    nnn
Desc:       a Accomp:      Dat tp:    s Dates: 1969,
 1 040       XXX ǂc XXX
 2 090       CC75
 3 092 0     930.10283 ǂ2 20
 4 049       XXXX
 5 100 1     Lipetzky, Jerry.
 6 245 10    Dig ǂh game : ǂb a simulation of the archeological
reconstruction of a vanished civilization / ǂc Jerry Lipetzky.
 7 260       Lakeside, Calif. : ǂb Interact, ǂc c1969.
 8 300       1 game (various pieces) ; ǂc bound in booklet (34 p. ;
28 cm.) + 30 identical student guides.
 9 500       Teacher's guide has directions for making artifacts
and for the educational simulation and includes pages to be
reproduced to use in the simulation.
10 520       Each of two teams creates a secret culture and makes
artifacts which are excavated by the other team; a confrontation
between teams reveals the accuracy of each reconstruction and
analysis.
11 650  0    Archaeology.
12 650  0    Simulation games in education.
13 650  8    Archeology.
14 650  8    Excavations (Archeology)
15 710 21    Interact (Firm)
```

There is no longer a second indicator in the 1XX field in any format; this is an early move toward format integration.

Example 85A: The Numbrella Tree (individual box)

```
Type:       r Bib lvl: m Source:    d Lang:  eng
Type mat: g Enc lvl: I Govt pub:   Ctry:  ohu
Int lvl:  b Mod rec:   Tech:      n Leng:  nnn
Desc:       a Accomp:     Dat tp:  s Dates: 1978,
 1 040      XXX ǂc XXX
 2 090      QA115
 3 092 0    513 ǂ2 20
 4 049      XXXX
 5 245 04   The Numbrella tree. ǂn A, ǂp Checked ǂh game
 6 260      Columbus, Ohio : ǂb Xerox Education Publications, ǂc
c1978.
 7 300      20 games : ǂb col. ; ǂc in box, 23 x 29 x 8 cm.
 8 440  0   Math skills games
 9 440  4   The game tree series
10 500      Game boards open to 28 x 44 cm. Set includes markers,
cards, spinners, instructions.
11 520      Designed to promote the development of basic
mathematical skills in grade 2 students.
12 650  0   Arithmetic.
13 650  8   Arithmetic.
14 710 21   Xerox Education Publications.
```

Field 245 coding is subfield ǂn for "number" of the part, ǂp for title of the part.

Example 85B: The Numbrella Tree (set)

```
Type:       r Bib lvl: m Source:    d Lang:  eng
Type mat: g Enc lvl: I Govt pub:   Ctry:  ohu
Int lvl:  c Mod rec:   Tech:      n Leng:  nnn
Desc:       a Accomp:     Dat tp:  s Dates: 1978,
 1 040      XXX ǂc XXX
 2 090      QA115
 3 092 0    513 ǂ2 20
 4 049      XXXX
 5 245 04   The Numbrella tree ǂh game : ǂb math skills games.
 6 260      Columbus, Ohio : ǂb Xerox Education Publications, ǂc
c1978.
 7 300      4 boxes of games : ǂb col. ; ǂc each box 23 x 29 x 8
cm.
 8 440  4   The game tree series
 9 505  0   A. Checked (grade 2) -- B. Striped (grade 3) -- C.
Polka-dot (grade 4) -- D. Plaid (grade 5).
10 650  0   Arithmetic.
11 650  8   Arithmetic.
12 710 21   Xerox Education Publications.
```

"Tech" and "Lang" are not used except for motion pictures and videorecordings.

Example 86: Jigsaw Puzzle Post Card

```
Type:       r Bib lvl: m Source:    d Lang:    eng
Type mat: g Enc lvl: I Govt pub:    Ctry:    mau
Int lvl:  e Mod rec:   Tech:      n Leng:    nnn
Desc:       a Accomp:    Dat tp:    s Dates: 1983,
   1 040      XXX ‡c XXX
   2 090      GV1507.J5
   3 092 0    793.73 ‡2 20
   4 049      XXXX
   5 245 00   Jigsaw puzzle post card ‡h game
   6 260      Newton, Mass. : ‡b Whitehall Games, ‡c [1983].
   7 300      1 jigsaw puzzle (15 pieces) : ‡b cardboard, col. ; ‡c
17 x 13 cm.
   8 500      Photograph by Anne Day of one of the corridors in the
Thomas Jefferson Building of the Library of Congress.
   9 650  0   Jigsaw puzzles.
* 10 610 20   Library of Congress Thomas Jefferson Building
  (Washington, D.C.)
  11 650  8   Puzzles.
  12 700 11   Day, Anne.
  13 710 21   Whitehall Games, Inc.
```

Fixed field "Int lvl" is coded "e" for adult. It is not particularly useful in this case.

Example 87: Minneapolis/St. Paul Scene

```
Type:       r Bib lvl: m Source:    d Lang:   eng
Type mat: g Enc lvl: I Govt pub:    Ctry:   cau
Int lvl:  g Mod rec:    Tech:     n Leng:   nnn
Desc:       a Accomp:    Dat tp:   s Dates: 1981,
  1 040      XXX ‡c XXX
  2 043      n-us-mn
  3 090      F614.M6 ‡a GV1469.M4
  4 092 0    917 ‡2 20
  5 049      XXXX
  6 245 00   Minneapolis/St. Paul scene ‡h game
  7 260      Milbrae, CA : ‡b John N. Hansen Co., ‡c c1981.
  8 300      1 game (various pieces) : ‡b col. ; ‡c in box 27 x 52
x 4 cm.
  9 520      A game for two to four players in which the players
try to accumulate wealth through buying and developing property,
gaining power, and acquiring connections. All properties, etc.,
represent actual places and companies from Minneapolis and St.
Paul, Minn. Game board is photo from space of the Twin Cities
area.
 10 650   0  Games.
 11 651   0  Minneapolis (Minn.)
 12 651   0  Saint Paul (Minn.)
 13 650   8  Board games.
 14 650   8  Games.
* 15 710 21  John N. Hansen Company, Inc.
```

Fixed field "Int lvl" here is coded "g" for general. It is usually used for fiction, but it seemed the best choice here.

Example 88: Froglegs Bean Bag

```
Type:       r Bib lvl: m Source:    d Lang:   eng
Type mat: g Enc lvl: I Govt pub:    Ctry:   ko
Int lvl:  b Mod rec:    Tech:     n Leng:   nnn
Desc:       a Accomp:    Dat tp:   q Dates: 1975,1979
  1 040      XXX ‡c XXX
  2 090      GV1218.B3
  3 092 0    688.72 ‡2 20
  4 049      XXXX
  5 245 00   Froglegs bean bag ‡h toy
** 6 260     San Francisco : ‡b [Distributed by] R. Dakin, ‡c
[between 1975 and 1979] ‡e (Korea)
  7 300      1 bean bag : ‡b fabric, green and white ; ‡c 27 cm.
long.
  8 440   0  Dakin bean bags
  9 500      Recommended for 3 years and up.
 10 650   0  Toys.
 11 650   8  Toys.
```

"Ctry" is coded for country of production rather than of distribution.

Example 89: Frog Hand Puppet

```
Type:       r Bib lvl: m Source:    d Lang:    eng
Type mat: g Enc lvl: I Govt pub:    Ctry:    txu
Int lvl:  b Mod rec:    Tech:     n Leng:    nnn
Desc:       a Accomp:    Dat tp:    s Dates: 1979,
  1 040       XXX ǂc XXX
  2 090       PN1972
  3 092 0     791.53 ǂ2 20
  4 049       XXXX
  5 245 00    [Frog hand puppet] ǂh toy
  6 260       [1979?] ǂe (Austin, Texas : ǂf Nancy Renfro Studios)
  7 300       2 puppets : ǂb fabric, col.
  8 500       Title supplied by cataloger.
  9 520       Yellow insect finger puppet (7 cm. long) attached by
elastic to green and pink frog hand puppet (27 cm. wide); designed
to be used with story or rhyme about a frog eating a fly.
*10 650  0    Puppets.
 11 650  8    Puppets and puppet-plays.
 12 710 21    Nancy Renfro Studios.
```

Date of distribution, place, and name of manufacturer are coded in field 260.

Example 90: Pac Man

```
Type:       r Bib lvl: m Source:    d Lang:    eng
Type mat: g Enc lvl: I Govt pub:    Ctry:    cau
Int lvl:  d Mod rec:    Tech:     n Leng:    nnn
Desc:       a Accomp:    Dat tp:    s Dates: 1981,
  1 040       XXX ǂc XXX
  2 090       GV1469.2
  3 092 0     794.8 ǂ2 20
  4 049       XXXX
  5 245 00    Tomytronic Pac Man ǂh game
  6 260       Carson, CA : ǂb Tomy Corp., ǂc c1981 ǂe (Japan)
  7 300       1 game : ǂb plastic, yellow and black ; ǂc 20 cm.
diam. x 6 cm. high in container, 22 x 22 x 8 cm.
  8 500       Electronic game in which player controls movement of
Pac Man as it eats bait, cherries, and monsters before the
monsters eat it. Player can choose between amateur (slow) or
professional (fast) versions.
  9 650  0    Electronic toys.
 10 650  8    Electronic toys.
 11 740 01    Pac Man.
```

All the dimensions go in a single subfield ǂc in field 300.

Example 91: The Quest for the Rings

```
Type:       r Bib lvl: m Source:    d Lang:   eng
Type mat: g Enc lvl: I Govt pub:    Ctry:   cau
Int lvl:  g Mod rec:   Tech:      n Leng:   nnn
Desc:       a Accomp:    Dat tp:   s Dates: 1981,
 1 040      XXX ǂc XXX
 2 090      GV1202.F35
 3 092 0    793.932 ǂb 20
 4 049      XXXX
 5 245 04   The Quest for the rings ǂh game
 6 260      [Los Angeles] : ǂb North American Philips Consumer
Electronics, ǂc c1982.
 7 300      1 computer chip cartridge, game board, game tokens,
keyboard overlay, direction booklet ; ǂc in container 20 x 26 x 6
cm.
 8 500      Game for 2-5 players.
 9 500      System requirements: Odyssey2 videogame system; color
TV.
10 500      Software copyright by E. Averett.
11 520      Players choose roles as wizard, warrior, changeling,
or phantom and attempt to recover 10 rings of power. Players move
through mazes on video screen (with sound and color) as they
gather items hidden in the maze enabling them to move on the
board.
12 650  0   Video games.
13 650  8   Video games.
14 700 11   Averett, E.
15 710 21   North American Philips Consumer Electronics Corp.
```

There is no field 538 or 753 in this format. After format integration one will be able to use whatever fields and codes are needed.

Example 92: Cannon Ball

```
Type:       r Bib lvl: m Source:    d Lang:   N/A
Type mat: g Enc lvl: I Govt pub:    Ctry:   xxu
Int lvl:  f Mod rec:   Tech:      n Leng:   nnn
Desc:       a Accomp:    Dat tp:    q Dates: 1861,1865
 1 040       XXX ǂc XXX
 2 043       n-us---
 3 045       w6w6
 4 090       E468.9
 5 092 0     623.42 ǂ2 20
 6 049       XXXX
 7 245 00    [Cannon ball] ǂh realia
 8 260       ǂe ([United states : ǂf s.n., ǂg 186-])
 9 300       1 cannon ball : ǂb lead, gray ; ǂc 10 cm. in diam.
10 500       Title supplied by cataloger.
11 520       "12-pounder" cannon ball used in the Civil War.
12 650  0    Ordnance.
13 651  0    United States ǂx History ǂy Civil War, 1861-1865.
14 650  8    Ordnance.
15 651  8    United States ǂx History ǂy 1861-1865, Civil War.
```

Field 043 for geographic access and field 045 for time period are both used here.

Example 93: Forget-Me-Not Toothpick Holder

```
Type:       r Bib lvl: m Source:    d Lang:   eng
Type mat: r Enc lvl: I Govt pub:    Ctry:   ohu
Int lvl:  g Mod rec:   Tech:      n Leng:   nnn
Desc:       a Accomp:    Dat tp:    q Dates: 1972,1965
 1 040       XXX ǂc XXX
 2 090       NK9508
 3 092 0     748.8 ǂ2 20
 4 049       XXXX
 5 245 00    [Forget-me-not toothpick holder] ǂh realia
 6 260       ǂc [1973] ǂe ([Cambridge, Ohio : ǂf Degenhart Crystal
Art Glass, ǂg between 1965 and 1972])
 7 300       1 toothpick holder : ǂb glass, bittersweet orange ; ǂc
6 cm. diam. x 6.3 cm. high.
** 8 500     Reproduction of 1899 U.S. Glass Co. pattern Vermont;
height slightly different from original.
 9 500       Title supplied by cataloger.
10 500       On paper sticker: D (in a heart).
11 650  0    Toothpick holders.
12 710 21    Degenhart Crystal Art Glass (Firm)
```

In field 260 the manufacturing date is coded in subfield ǂg, the date of distribution is coded in subfield ǂc.

Example 94: Cow Pull Toy

```
Type:       r Bib lvl: m Source:     d Lang:  eng
Type mat: r Enc lvl: I Govt pub:     Ctry:  ohu
Int lvl:  b Mod rec:    Tech:      n Leng:  nnn
Desc:       a Accomp:     Dat tp:   s Dates: 1982,
 1 040      XXX ‡c XXX
 2 090      GV1218.P8
 3 092 0    688.72 ‡2 20
 4 049      XXXX
 5 100 1    Hardy, Margaret.
 6 245 10   [Cow pull toy] ‡h realia / ‡c Margaret Hardy.
 7 260      ‡c 1982 ‡e (Trinway, Ohio)
 8 300      1 toy : ‡b wood, natural ; ‡c 26 x 34 x 16 cm.
 9 500      Wooden model of a cow mounted on wheeled base with
string and handle for child to pull.
10 500      Title supplied by cataloger.
11 500      Signed and dated on bottom of base.
12 650  0   Wooden toys.
13 650  8   Toys.
```

This was dated, so I used that date as a single date in the fixed field.

Example 95: Tree-of-Life Candleholder

```
Type:       r Bib lvl: m Source:     d Lang:  eng
Type mat: z Enc lvl: I Govt pub:     Ctry:  mx
Int lvl:  g Mod rec:    Tech:      n Leng:  nnn
Desc:       a Accomp:     Dat tp:   s Dates: 1981,
 1 040      XXX ‡c XXX
 2 043      n-mx---
 3 090      BL444
 4 092 0    745.5933 ‡2 20
 5 049      XXXX
 6 245 00   [Tree-of-life candleholder]
 7 260      ‡c [1981?] ‡e (Mexico)
 8 300      1 candleholder : ‡b clay, tan ; ‡c 26 cm. high.
 9 500      Handmade sculpture of tree of life with two candle
sockets and death's head at top, serpent in tree, Eve offering
Adam apple near base.
10 500      Title supplied by cataloger.
11 500      Paper sticker under base: Made in Mexico.
12 650  0   Tree of life.
13 650  0   Folk art ‡x Mexico.
14 650  8   Folk art ‡x Mexico.
```

A mark of punctuation at the beginning of field 245 can be ignored in coding the filing indicator unless it appears with an initial article.

Example 96: Pot

```
Type:       r Bib lvl: m Source:    d Lang:    eng
Type mat:   r Enc lvl: I Govt pub:    Ctry:    nmu
Int lvl:    g Mod rec:    Tech:     n Leng:    nnn
Desc:       a Accomp:     Dat tp:   q Dates:  1963,1965
   1 040        XXX ǂc XXX
   2 090        E98.P8
   3 092  0     738.38 ǂ2 20
   4 049        XXXX
*  5 100  1     Mart´inez, Mar´ia Montoya.
   6 245 10     [Pot] ǂh realia / ǂc Maria & Santana.
   7 260        ǂc [196-?]
   8 300        1 pot : ǂc clay, black ; ǂc 12 cm. diam. x 7 cm. high.
   9 500        Piece of pottery made by Maria, decorated by her son
Santana, both of San Ildefonso Pueblo, N.M.
  10 500        Purchased in 1965 in Santa Fe, N.M.
  11 500        Signed in pencil on base.
  12 650  0     Pueblo Indians ǂx Pottery.
  13 650  8     Pottery, Indian.
  14 650  8     Pueblo Indians ǂx Art.
* 15 700 11     Mart´inez, Santana.
```

I assume this was made shortly before I purchased it in 1965, so I coded "Dat tp" as "q" for questionable and guessed it was made not before 1963.

Example 97: Nativity Set

```
Type:       r Bib lvl: m Source:    d Lang:    N/A
Type mat:   d Enc lvl: I Govt pub:    Ctry:    ohu
Int lvl:    g Mod rec:    Tech:     n Leng:    nnn
Desc:       a Accomp:     Dat tp:   s Dates:  1982
   1 040        XXX ǂc XXX
   2 090        N8060
   3 092  0     232.921 ǂ2 20
   4 049        XXXX
   5 100  1     Robbin, Betty.
   6 245 10     [Nativity set]
   7 260        ǂc [1982]
   8 300        12 figures : ǂc yarn, col. ; ǂc tallest 28 cm.
   9 500        Crocheted figures stuffed with batting; made by Betty
Robbin, Columbus, Ohio.
  10 500        Title supplied by cataloger.
  11 600 00     Jesus Christ ǂx Art.
  12 600 08     Jesus Christ ǂx Nativity.
```

"Lang" is coded "N/A" because there is no writing anywhere on this set of figures.

MICROFORMS

AACR 2 Chapter 11

Example 98: Photography by the Wright Brothers

```
Type: a Bib lvl: m Source:    d Lang:   eng
Repr:    Enc lvl: I Conf pub: 0 Ctry:   dcu
Indx: 0 Mod rec:    Govt pub: f Cont:
Desc: a Int lvl:    Festschr: 0 Illus: a
        F/B:      0 Dat tp:   s Dates: 1978,
 1 010     78-606137
 2 040     XXX ǂc XXX
 3 020     0844402664
 4 007     h ǂb e ǂd a ǂe m ǂf u— ǂg b ǂh u ǂi c ǂj a
 5 043     n-us—
 6 045     w8x1
 7 050     TL521
 8 082 00  629.130092 ǂ2 20
 9 090     TL521
10 049     XXXX
11 100 1   Wright, Wilbur, ǂd 1867-1912.
12 245 10  Photographs by the Wright Brothers ǂh microform : ǂb
prints from the glass negatives in the Library of Congress.
13 260     Washington, D.C. : ǂb Library of Congress ; For sale
by the Supt. of Docs., U.S. G.P.O., ǂc 1978.
14 300     5 microfiches : ǂb all ill. + ǂe 1 guide (20 p. : ill.
; 19 cm.)
15 500     "A micropublication commemorating the seventy-fifth
anniversary of the first flight by the Wright Brothers, December
17, 1903"--Cover of guide.
16 500     Prints of each negative are available from the Library
of Congress.
17 650  0  Aeronautics ǂz United States ǂx History.
18 600 10  Wright, Orville, ǂd 1871-1948.
19 600 10  Wright, Wilbur, ǂd 1867-1912.
20 650  8  Airplanes ǂx History.
21 700 1   Wright, Orville, ǂd 1871-1948.
```

Field 007 is used for microforms.

For all examples —

* Changed from form appearing in *Cataloging of Audiovisual Materials*, 3d edition. LC authority file searched June 1992.

** Cataloging changed.

Example 99: Pottery Techniques

```
Type: a Bib lvl: m Source:    d Lang:   eng
Repr:    Enc lvl: I Conf pub: 0 Ctry:   ilu
Indx: 0 Mod rec:    Govt pub:    Cont:
Desc: a Int lvl:    Festschr: 0 Illus: a
        F/B:       0 Dat tp:    s Dates: 1976,
 1 040       XXX ǂc XXX
 2 020       0226698157
 3 007       h ǂb e ǂd a ǂe m ǂf u— ǂg c ǂh u ǂi c ǂj a
 4 043       n-us—
 5 090       E98.P8
 6 092  0    738.14089975 ǂ2 20
 7 049       XXXX
 8 100  1    White, John Kennardh.
 9 245 10    Pottery techniques of native North America ǂh
microform : ǂb an introduction to traditional technology / ǂc John
Kennardh White ; photographs by Stewart J. Macleod.
10 260       Chicago : ǂb University of Chicago Press, ǂc c1976.
11 300       4 microfiches (336 fr.) : ǂb all col. ill ; ǂc 11 x 15
cm. + ǂe 1 manual (52 p. : ill. ; 21 cm.).
12 440  2    A University of Chicago Press text/fiche
13 520       Shows how to duplicate several Cherokee pots and bowls
using techniques developed by Cherokee potters. Shows many
examples of pottery made by Indians in the southeast United
States.
14 650  0    Cherokee Indians ǂx Pottery.
15 650  0    Indians of North America ǂx Pottery.
16 650  8    Pottery, Indian ǂx Technique.
17 650  8    Cherokee Indians ǂx Art.
18 700 11    MacLeod, Stewart J.
```

A filing indicator is used with field 440.

Example 100: The Architecture of Washington, D.C.

```
Type: a Bib lvl: m Source:    d Lang:   eng
Repr:    Enc lvl: I Conf pub: 0 Ctry:   dcu
Indx: 0 Mod rec:    Govt pub: f Cont:
Desc: a Int lvl:    Festschr: 0 Illus: a
        F/B:     0 Dat tp:   m Dates: 1976,9999
 1 040      XXX ‡c XXX
 2 020      0894810014 (v. 1)
 3 007      h ‡b e ‡d a ‡e m ‡f u— ‡g b ‡h u ‡i c ‡j a
 4 043      n-us—
 5 090      NA735.W5
 6 092 0    720.9753 ‡2 20
 7 049      XXXX
 8 245 04   The Architecture of Washington, D.C. ‡h microform / ‡c
Bates Lowry, editor.
 9 260      Washington, D.C. : ‡b Dunlap Society ; ‡a Essex, N.Y.
: ‡b Visual Documentation Program [distributor], ‡c 1976-
10 300         microfiches : ‡b ill. ; ‡c 11 x 15 cm. + ‡e
pages of introductory material.
11 500      Introductory material also on first frames of
microfiche.
12 500      Also available as slides (b&w or col.) or photographic
prints.
13 520      For each building includes all known early drawings,
prints, and photographs of the setting, interior, and exterior, as
well as selected construction drawings and photographs.
14 505 0    v. 1. The White House (10 microfiches). The Octagon (2
microfiches). Treasury Building (4 microfiches). General Post
Office (2 microfiches). Washington Monument (3 microfiches).
State, War, and Navy Building (5 microfiches). Pension Building (2
microfiches). Union Station (4 microfiches). Lincoln Memorial (4
microfiches). Supreme Court Building (4 microfiches) -- v. 2. The
United States Capitol (21 microfiches). Patent Office building (4
microfiches). Smithsonian Institution Building (4 microfiches).
Library of Congress (5 microfiches). Pan American Union Building
(4 microfiches). The Federal Triangle (8 microfiches). Jefferson
Memorial (2 microfiches).
15 650  0   Architecture ‡z Washington (D.C.) ‡x History.
16 651  0   Washington (D.C.) ‡x Buildings, structures, etc.
17 651  8   Washington, D.C. ‡x Historic buildings.
18 700 11   Lowry, Bates, ‡d 1923-
19 710 21   Dunlap Society.
```

In the fixed field, multiple dates are coded for this ongoing monographic series.

AUDIOVISUAL SERIALS

AACR 2 Chapter 12

Example 101: News Program

```
Type:     a Bib lvl: s Source:   d Lang:    eng
Repr:       Enc lvl: I Govt pub:   Ctry:    iau
Phys med: z Mod rec:   Conf pub: 0 Cont:    ^^^^
S/L ent:  0 Ser tp:  p Frequn:   w Alphabt: a
Desc:     a             Regulr:   n ISDS:
                        Pub st:   u Dates:   1950,9999
 1 040       XXX ǂc XXX
 2 090       D421
 3 092 0     909.82805 ǂ2 20
 4 049       XXXX
 5 245 00    News program ǂh filmstrip
 6 246 33    News lesson.
 7 260       Dubuque, Ia. : ǂb Visual Education Center, ǂc 1950-
 8 300          filmstrips : ǂb b&w ; ǂc 35 mm. + ǂe    teacher's
guides + semester quizzes.
 9 362 0     Vol. 1, no. 1 (Sept. 7, 1950)-
10 310       Weekly during the school year.
11 500       Title on container: News lesson.
12 520       Pictures from the news of the week are presented with
discussion questions.
13 650   0   History ǂx Study and teaching (Elementary)
14 650   8   Current events ǂx Periodicals.
15 650   8   Historiography ǂx Periodicals.
16 710 21    Visual Education Center.
```

This is shown on a serials workform. The AV workform allows coding of the visual materials details while the serial workform permits coding of the serials information. After format integration one will be able to code both types of information on one workform.

"Frequen" is coded "w" as the closest value. Field 007 is used in the serials format only for microforms. "Phys med" is coded "z"; multimedia value is only to be used for a serial kit.

The display constant "Summary:" is generated from the blank first indicator in the 520 field.

For all examples —

* Changed from form appearing in *Cataloging of Audiovisual Materials*, 3d edition. LC authority file searched June 1992.

** Cataloging changed.

Example 102: Pediatrics

```
Type:     i Bib lvl: m Source: d  Lang:  eng
Repr:       Enc lvl: I Format: n  Ctry:  cau
Accomp:     Mod rec:  Comp:   nn  LTxt:  1
Desc:     a Int lvl:  Dat tp: m  Dates: 1960,9999
 1 040       XXX ǂc XXX
 2 007       s ǂb s ǂd l ǂe m ǂf n ǂg j ǂh l ǂi b
 3 090       RJ1
 4 092 0     618.920005 ǂ2 20
 5 049       XXXX
 6 245 00    Pediatrics ǂh sound recording
 7 260       Glendale, Calif. : ǂb Audio-Digest Foundation,
 8 300         sound cassettes : ǂb analog + ǂe   guides.
 9 500       Description based on: Vol. 12, no. 1.
10 500       Frequency varies: 24 or 48 nos. per volume.
11 500       Some numbers on sound tape reels.
12 500       Index issued for each volume.
13 650  0    Pediatrics ǂx Periodicals.
14 650  8    Children ǂx Diseases ǂx Periodicals.
15 710 21    Audio-Digest Foundation.
```

This is done on the sound recording workform.

Example 103: Audiology

```
Type:     i Bib lvl: m Source: d  Lang:  eng
Repr:       Enc lvl: I Format: n  Ctry:  nyu
Accomp:     Mod rec:  Comp:   nn  LTxt:  1
Desc:     a Int lvl:  Dat tp: m  Dates: 1976,1981
 1 040       XXX ǂc XXX
 2 007       s ǂb s ǂd l ǂe m ǂf n ǂg j ǂh l ǂi b
 3 090       RF290
 4 092 0     617.8005 ǂ2 20
 5 049       XXXX
 6 245 00    Audiology ǂh sound recording : ǂb an audio journal for
continuing education.
 7 250       Vol. 1, no. 1-v. 6, no. 12.
 8 260       New York : ǂb Grune & Stratton, ǂc 1976-1981.
 9 300       7 v. (84 sound cassettes) : ǂb analog + ǂe 84 printed
guides.
10 500       Monthly.
11 500       Continued by: Audiology (published in hard copy).
12 500       Each volume in a binder; printed contents list issued
annually.
13 650  0    Audiology ǂx Periodicals.
14 650  8    Hearing ǂx Periodicals.
15 710 21    Grune & Stratton.
```

Field 250 was used for area 3 because this is the only way to get the information printed on cards in the proper place when using the sound recording format.

Example 104: Softdisk magazette.

```
Type:      m Bib lvl: s Source:    d Lang:    eng
File:      b Enc lvl: I Govt pub:   Ctry:    lau
Audience: d Mod rec:   Frequn:   m Regulr: r
Desc:      a            Pub st:   c Dates:   1981,9999
 1 040      XXX ‡c XXX
 2 090      QA75.5
 3 092 0    005.105 ‡2 20
 4 049      XXXX
 5 245 00   Softdisk magazette ‡h computer file
 6 260      Shreveport, La. : ‡b Softdisk magazette,
 7 300          computer disks : sd., col. ; ‡c 5 1/4 in.
 8 310      Monthly
 9 362 1    Began publication Sept. 1981.
10 538      System requirements: Apple II or higher.
11 500      Description based on: Aug. 1982; title from disk
label.
12 650  0  Programming (Electronic computers) ‡x Periodicals.
13 650  8  Programming (Electronic computers) ‡x Periodicals.
```

This format permits both serial and monograph cataloging of the material. The note "Monthly" can be generated from the fixed field value "Frequn:".

Example 105: Congressional Masterfile

```
Type:        m Bib lvl: s Source:    d Lang:    eng
File:        m Enc lvl: I Govt pub:   Ctry:    mdu
Audience: f Mod rec:   Frequn:   q Regulr: r
Desc:        a             Pub st:    c Dates:  1989,9999
  1 040      XXX ‡c XXX
  2 090      QA75.5
  3 092 0    005.105 ‡2 20
  4 049      XXXX
  5 245 00   Congressional masterfile 2 ‡h computer file
  6 260      Bethesda, MD : ‡b Congressional Information Service,
‡c 1989-
  7 300         computer disks ; ‡c 4 3/4 in. + ‡e 1 computer disk
(3 1/2 in.) + 1 user's manual.
  8 362 0    1970-
  9 310      Quarterly
 10 500      "CIS/index to congressional publications and
legislative histories."
 11 538      System requirements: IBM PC or compatible; hard disk
drive; 640K; CD-ROM drive with Microsoft extensions.
 12 500      Title from disk label.
 13 500      First CD-ROM covers 1970-1982; second disk, 1983-
replaced quarterly.
 14 500      Description based on: 1970-1982, 1983-Mar. 1991.
 15 651  0   United States. ‡b Congress ‡x Committees ‡x Indexes.
 16 650  8   Legislative hearings ‡x United States ‡x Indexes.
 17 651  0   United States ‡x Politics and government ‡x Indexes.
** 18 650  0   Government publications ‡z United States ‡x Indexes.
 19 710 20   Congressional Information Service.
 20 740  0   Congressional masterfile.
```

KITS AND OTHER PROBLEMS

Example 106: Immigrant Experience

```
Type:      o Bib lvl: m Source:    d Lang:   eng
Type mat: b Enc lvl: I Govt pub:    Ctry:   mnu
Int lvl:  f Mod rec:   Tech:      n Leng:   nnn
Desc:      a Accomp:     Dat tp:  s Dates: 1979,
 1 040       XXX ǂc XXX
 2 007       g ǂb o ǂd c ǂe n ǂg b ǂg d ǂh f
 3 043       n-us-mn
 4 045       x5w7
 5 090       F606
 6 092 0     325.776 ǂ2 20
 7 049       XXXX
 8 245 04  The Immigrant experience ǂh kit : ǂb a Minnesota
history resource unit / ǂc produced by the Education Division,
Minnesota Historical Society.
 9 260       St. Paul, Minn. : ǂb The Society, ǂc c1979.
10 300       8 filmstrips, 4 sound discs, 10 biography banners, 1
intermediate booklet, 30 identical copies of secondary booklet, 1
teacher's guide, 1 set of resource materials ; ǂc in box 34 x 34 x
34 cm.
11 500       Resource materials include reproductions of tickets,
posters, ship manifests, blueprint of Ellis Island, maps, census
schedules, birth, death, and marriage certificates, and time line;
teacher's guide includes scripts of sound filmstrips.
12 520       Designed to present intermediate and secondary
students with a historical account of the migration and
immigration of people to Minnesota, with particular emphasis on
the nineteenth and twentieth centuries.
13 651  0  Minnesota ǂx Emigration and immigration.
14 651  0  Minnesota ǂx History ǂy 1858-
15 650  8  Immigration and emigration.
16 651  8  Minnesota ǂx History.
17 651  8  United States ǂx Immigration and emigration.
18 710 21  Minnesota Historical Society. ǂb Education Division.
```

Kits are cataloged with value "o" for "Type" and value "b" for "Type mat" in the fixed field. Field 007 is for the sound filmstrips.

For all examples —

* Changed from form appearing in *Cataloging of Audiovisual Materials*, 3d edition. LC authority file searched June 1992.

** Cataloging changed.

Example 107: World War I

```
Type:        o Bib lvl: m Source:    d Lang:   eng
Type mat: b Enc lvl: I Govt pub:    Ctry:   flu
Int lvl:  f Mod rec:   Tech:      n Leng:   nnn
Desc:     a Accomp:    Dat tp:    s Dates: 1982,
 1 040       XXX ǂc XXX
 2 020       0897770153
 3 043       n-us---
 4 045       x1x1
 5 090       D570.A35
 6 092 0     973.913 ǂ2 19
 7 049       XXXX
 8 245 00    World War I ǂh kit : ǂb the home front.
 9 260       Boca Raton, Fl. : ǂb National Archives and SirS, ǂc
[1982?]
10 300       4 posters, 1 chart, 12 reproductions of photographs, 2
news sheets, 28 reproductions of documents, 1 teacher's guide ; ǂc
in box 37 x 23 x 2 cm.
11 500       "A supplemental teaching unit from the records of the
National Archives"--Teacher's guide.
12 500       Teacher's guide includes bibliography, exercises,
worksheets, glossary, time line.
13 505 0     America moves toward war -- Women and the war effort -
- Uncle Sam needs you -- Reactions to the call -- When Johnny
comes marching home.
14 650  0    World War, 1914-1918 ǂz United States.
15 651  0    United States ǂx History ǂy 1913-1921.
16 650  8    World War, 1914-1918 ǂz United States.
17 710 21    Social Issues Resources Series, Inc.
18 710 21    National Archives Trust Fund Board.
```

The ISBN is entered in field 020, just as for books.

Example 108: Secrets From the Past

```
Type:       o Bib lvl: m Source:    d Lang:    eng
Type mat: b Enc lvl: I Govt pub:   Ctry:     dcu
Int lvl:  d Mod rec:   Tech:     n Leng:    nnn
Desc:       a Accomp:    Dat tp:   s Dates:  1979,
 1 040       XXX ǂc XXX
 2 090       CC100
 3 092 0     930.1 ǂ2 20
 4 049       XXXX
 5 245 00    Secrets from the past ǂh kit
 6 260       Washington, D.C. : ǂb National Geographic Society, ǂc
c1979.
 7 300       1 book, 1 poster, 2 games, 8 duplicating masters, 1
activity booklet.
 8 500       Text of book (104 p.) by Gene S. Stuart.
 9 500       Gameboards on back of poster.
10 520       Introduces young people to the field of archaeology
through stories of discoveries made by children, stories of
youngsters who were influential in ancient times, and stories
recreating childhood experiences from other times and cultures.
11 500       Games: Senet -- Snakes and ladders.
12 650   0   Archaeology.
13 650   8   Archeology.
14 700 12    Stuart, Gene S. ǂt Secrets from the past. ǂf 1979.
15 710 21    National Geographic Society (U.S.)
16 730 01    Senet. ǂf 1979.
17 730 01    Snakes and ladders. ǂf 1979.
```

Field 300 is entered in a single subfield ǂa.

Line 11 is really a partial contents note, but if we used field 505 with first indicator "2" it would generate the print constant "Partial contents:" and we don't want that.

Example 109: Step by Step Two

```
Type:       o Bib lvl: m Source:    d Lang:   eng
Type mat: b Enc lvl: I Govt pub:   Ctry:   ctu
Int lvl:  f Mod rec:   Tech:    n Leng:   nnn
Desc:       a Accomp:    Dat tp:   s Dates: 1983,
 1 040      XXX ‡c XXX
 2 007      s ‡b s ‡d l ‡e m ‡f n ‡g j ‡h l ‡i b
 3 090      QA76.73.B3
 4 092  0   005.262 ‡2 20
 5 049      XXXX
 6 245 00   Step by step two ‡h kit : ‡b an intermediate course in
BASIC programming.
 7 260      Greenwich, CT : ‡b Program Design, ‡c c1983.
 8 300      4 sound cassettes, 2 computer disks, 1 workbook ; ‡c
in container 30 x 26 x 5 cm.
 9 500      System requirements: Apple II computer.
10 500      Title on cassettes: Step by step 2.
11 500      Project designer, John Victor ; programmers, Stephen
Chmielewski, Kathleen Fortmeier.
12 500      Continuation of: New step by step.
13 500      One disk is back-up.
14 520      Student uses computer while sound cassettes guide
student through each of five lessons.
15 650  0   BASIC (Computer program language)
16 650  8   Programming languages (Electronic computers) ‡x
Problems, exercises, etc.
17 650  8   BASIC (Computer programming language) ‡x Problems,
exercises, etc.
18 700 11   Victor, John.
19 700 11   Chmielewski, Stephen.
20 700 11   Fortmeier, Kathleen A.
21 710 21   Program Design, Inc.
22 740 01   Step by step 2.
```

This has a a field 007 for the sound cassettes.

Example 110: Speedy Andrew's Repair Shop (kit)

```
Type:      o Bib lvl: m Source:    d Lang:   eng
Type mat: b Enc lvl: I Govt pub:    Ctry:   nju
Int lvl:  g Mod rec:    Tech:     n Leng:   nnn
Desc:      a Accomp:    Dat tp:    s Dates: 1977,
  1 040        XXX ‡c XXX
  2 090        TL153
  3 092 0      629.286 ‡2 20
  4 049        XXXX
  5 245 00     Speedy Andrews' repair shop ‡h kit
  6 260        Moorestown, N.J. : ‡b Tyco Industries, ‡c c1977 ‡e
(West Germany : ‡f Pola)
  7 300        76 pieces ; ‡c in box 17 x 32 x 4 cm.
  8 440 0      Tycokit
  9 500        HO scale.
 10 500        "For ages 8 years and up."
 11 520        To be assembled into plastic model of automobile
repair shop of the 1920's.
*12 650 0      Service stations.
 13 650 8      Automobiles ‡x Service stations.
 14 710 21     Tyco Industries.
```

I coded fixed field "Int lvl" as "g" for general because these kits are used by all ages.

Example 111: The Real Mother Goose Piano Book

```
Type:    c Bib lvl: m Source: d  Lang:   eng
Repr:      Enc lvl: I Format:    Ctry:   nyu
Accomp:    Mod rec:   Comp:    sg LTxt:   n
Desc:    a Int lvl: j Dat tp: s  Dates:  1987,
  1 010
  2 040        XXX ‡c XXX
  3 020        0028995007
  4 090        M1992
  5 092 0      398.8 ‡2 20
  6 049        XXXX
  7 130 0      Mother Goose.
  8 245 14     The real Mother Goose piano book ‡h music / ‡c illustrated
by Blanche Fisher Wright.
  9 260        New York : ‡b Checkerboard Press, ‡c [1987?]
 10 300        [18] p. of music : ‡b col. ill. ; ‡c 29 cm. + ‡e 13-key
electronic piano.
 11 500        Nine nursery rhymes with piano accompaniment numbered for
attached electronic keyboard.
 12 650 0      Children's songs.
 13 650 0      Nursery rhymes.
 14 700 10     Wright, Blanche Fisher.
 15 710 20     Checkerboard Press.
```

This is entered on a scores workform.

Example 112: The Malinsay Massacre

```
Type: a Bib lvl: m Source:    d Lang:   eng
Repr:    Enc lvl: I Conf pub: 0 Ctry:   nyu
Indx: 0 Mod rec:    Govt pub:    Cont:
Desc: a Int lvl:    Festschr: 0 Illus: a
        F/B:      1 Dat tp:    r Dates: 1982,1938
 1 010
 2 040       XXX ǂc XXX
 3 020       0831757981 ǂc $ 17.95
 4 090       PR6045.H127
 5 092 0     823.912 ǂ2 20
 6 049       XXXX
 7 100 1     Wheatley, Dennis, ǂd 1897-1977.
 8 245 14    The Malinsay massacre / ǂc Dennis Wheatley presents a third
murder mystery planned by J.G. Links.
 9 260       New York, N.Y. : ǂb Rutledge Press, ǂc [1982?]
10 300       [105] leaves : ǂb ill. ; ǂc 27 cm.
11 500       Murder mystery with solution in sealed section at back of
book.
12 500       Cover title.
13 500       Contains "the complete file of the actual evidence including
letters, maps, press reports, and photographs"--Book jacket.
14 534       Reprint. ǂp Originally published: ǂc London : Rutledge
Press, 1938.
15 650  0    Detective and mystery stories, English.
16 700 10    Links, J. G. ǂq (Joseph Gluckstein), ǂd 1904-
```

Field 534 is a coded field citing the original work.